AUTHENTIC SELLING

How to boost your sales performance by being yourself

GUY ANASTAZE

Authentic Selling

First published in 2015 by

Panoma Press Ltd
48 St Vincent Drive, St Albans, Herts, AL1 5SJ, UK
info@panomapress.com
www.panomapress.com

Book layout by Neil Coe.

Printed on acid-free paper from managed forests.

ISBN 978-1-909623-98-9

The right of Guy Anastaze to be identified as the author of this work has been asserted in accordance with sections 77 and 78 of the Copyright Designs and Patents Act 1988.

A CIP catalogue record for this book is available from the British Library.

This book is available online and in bookstores.

To my daughters *Alexandra and Karine*
To my grandson *David*

May you live loving others, knowing why you do what you do,
depending neither on a person nor an ideology nor a habit
and simply feeling good about yourself.

TABLE OF CONTENTS

TESTIMONIALS

This book is about the positive psychology of selling and imaginatively integrates scientific foundations with a hands-on approach. Given the importance of selling in our everyday life, this is a must for every professional, whether officially in the sales force or not.

Dr. Ilona Boniwell
CEO, Positran
Director of International MSc in Applied Positive Psychology at Anglia Ruskin University, UK
Associate Professor at Ecole Centrale Paris, France

Through this book, Guy Anastaze brings together his experience in areas as diverse as human psychology and sales methodologies in a personal approach that is open to everyone, but places, above all, the human being at the center. While it is a reader that will open this book, it will be a seller who will turn the last page.

Marc Chikhani
CEO, SR Operations, Switzerland

Authentic Selling may be aimed at young salespeople, yet this rich collection of life experiences can speak to the hearts of us all. Sincere and generous, Guy provides us with a user's guide to success, happiness and serenity. I thank him for highlighting the Enneagram as a powerful tool for personal development.

Marie-Claire Fagioli,
Coaching and Enneagram teacher, owner of Moncoach.ch, Switzerland

As manager of the logistics center at a major banking group, I often have the opportunity to meet salespeople who have yet to read Guy Anastaze's book. This book is a prerequisite for all salespeople looking for tools and methods that will enable them to improve and increase the value they bring to their clients. In addition, this book provided me personally with very relevant answers to several questions I had asked myself when my professional development required me to make important choices.

Jean–Claude Favre,
Head of Crédit Agricole Private Banking Services, Switzerland

An excellent book that puts human beings and their values at the center of the action. The book addresses the important points and proposes alternatives to readers. The author revisits the fundamentals of true authentic selling, which allow you to enjoy and fully experience the art of selling.

Eric Guinchard
CEO, Wird, Switzerland

For anyone involved in a commercial activity it is critical that you take the chance to read Guy Anastaze's book. Thanks to his uncommon and demanding path, Guy has managed to re-discover the beauty of a very old job: making sure that demand and offer meet in the most positive, rewarding and uplifting experience for both. That's a true and invaluable gift for all salespeople which will find the way - and the relevant practice - to become proud of their job and even more importantly of who they become.

Olivier Piazza
Co-director Executive Coaching Master Program,
University of Cergy Pontoise, France

Authentic Selling may be primarily addressed to salespeople interested in or in need of boosting their sales performance, but it will also certainly appeal to any professional interested in personal development and a balanced and coherent way of life, leading to the optimization of one's own potential, and efficient and stimulating interaction with others. Guy Anastaze's sharing of his own personal experiences makes it all the more credible and likeable and serves as an introduction to a number of methods and approaches that are indeed worth exploring.

Alexandre Vassiltchikov
Member of the Executive Committee
CFO/CRO
ING Belgium, Geneva Branch, Switzerland

FOREWORD

Is selling an art or a science? Why is sales an unpopular profession? How can its nobility be restored? What makes a salesperson truly successful over the long-term? With the internet playing a more and more predominant role in business, what are the essential characteristics that will distinguish a salesperson as one of the best in their profession and make them a valued interlocutor sought after by their clients? If you are looking for the answer to these questions, this book is for you.

It is amazing that something that appears to be relatively simple – a sale – can actually turn into a difficult undertaking and a long journey. There are often many obstacles that a seller must overcome in order to be successful: fierce and varying competition, margin pressure, the emergence of new buyer groups, a product at the beginning or the end of its life cycle… which can lead to the dilemma of how to resist immense pressure, reach our ambitious goals and yet remain sincere, positive and calm?

As sellers, we are at the forefront. Educated on products and services, sales negotiation processes and tactics, buyer behavior and buying patterns, sales psychology and ethical business conduct. Sales techniques, sometimes taught in company training programs but mainly learned "on the job", constitute our basic knowledge. A sales attitude comes mainly from industry practices and company culture, and shapes a seller's know-how.

Each company reaches a point where performance is an issue and success is not coming as easily as before. Being able to react and respond to changing customer needs and sustain growth while improving profitability requires both sales culture and sales processes. Effectively addressing these challenges needs to be done through a combination of art and science, driven by the right mindset. Here enters the *savoir-être*, as presented by Guy Anastaze – a subtle mix of human skills and personal values that develops and cultivates the underlying personality of the seller year after year and plays a key role in sales success.

Thus, successful selling can be so easy, and yet so very difficult. What differentiates a successful seller, the winning sales team and the runner-up? Is it their appetite for success, the "never give up" mentality or simply a better product or better terms and conditions? Probably not one single factor, but a clever combination of all of these elements. From my point of view there are three key ingredients:

The art of listening – a successful seller knows when to be quiet and listen; a successful seller knows how to "read between the lines"; a successful seller knows about the "magic of silence". For this, a successful seller must demonstrate humility.

The art of asking the right questions – a successful seller listens and turns what he has heard into questions, a successful seller knows that most customers like to share their thoughts and guide us through the sales process; a successful seller knows about the power of asking the right questions. For this, a successful seller must demonstrate empathy.

The art of closing the contract – a successful seller knows when to ask for the client signature; a successful seller knows that time kills deals; a successful seller knows when the negotiations are over. For this, a successful seller must demonstrate leadership.

But, speaking from my own personal experience, the most important of all is your love for people and your genuine interest in them. Guy Anastaze has shared with clarity, conviction and simplicity why and how to master Authentic Selling because he is such a seller and person himself, as he has demonstrated for over three decades. I admire his passion for the customer and his positive persistence in doing what is right for his client, and in the end for the company he is representing.

I wish the reader an enlightening and rewarding journey through a new and inspiring vision of the art and science of selling – and lots of success from applying it in his daily life as a professional seller!

Edward Gaehwiler
Vice President, Enterprise Clients
Member of the Board, IBM Switzerland

HOW DID I GET HERE?
A LITTLE STORY ABOUT MYSELF

Two passions have been important to me since I was very young: mathematics and personal development. Mathematics is what allowed me to discover the secrets of theoretical physics and the beauty of symmetries underlying our universe models, and to lead research projects at the National Center for Scientific Research (CNRS) in Strasbourg, at the École Polytechnique in Palaiseau and at the University of Geneva. It gave me a taste for analytical rigor, for the use of these two fundamental questions *Why?* and *How?* and for the continuous questioning of my convictions. Mathematics gave me a strength: one of understanding, and a humility: one of not at *all* understanding. The result was a strong appetite for both learning and teaching because I cannot imagine one without the other.

My passion for personal development came from two experiences that took place during my childhood and adolescence.

The first one occurred when I was ten years old and I felt the fear of abduction. I lived in Buenos Aires in Argentina where we regularly witnessed urban violence. One day, the fear arrived and it was the type of fear that falls over you out of the blue and gnaws at you every moment. At first, I tried to rationalize the fear. Then, instinctively, I understood that I needed to conquer this fear with fear. So I looked for situations where this could take place, such as volunteering myself for my scout camp's night watch 200 meters deep in the forest. It took me two years to make the fear disappear. Alone. Without a word from anyone. I later said to myself that I would have liked to have talked to my parents, or at least to someone who could have reassured me, guided me and helped me overcome this fear. It certainly would have taken less than two years!

The second experience took place when I was about fourteen years old and I arrived a few minutes after a suicide had occurred on a railroad track that I crossed every day. The body was lying under newspapers and I could see a glimpse of a strangely positioned foot. At the time, I felt nothing, no emotion in particular. The next day, the gate lowered and I waited for the train to pass. When the train arrived, I started to tremble violently, in my arms and upper body. I then decided to go there every evening to wait for the train. The trembling disappeared within a week.

These two challenges showed me how strong our hidden resources are. The first lesson I learned was that *we have to love ourselves because we are the person with whom we must live the longest*.

The second lesson was that when we *really* want to do something, we *really* can. Life has taught me that this rule is not simple to follow and that *failure is not in falling, it is in not getting up*.

My passion for personal development was first expressed in the need to educate myself in various subjects (a University Diploma in Executive Coaching from the University of Cergy Pontoise, a Coaching and Enneagram Certification, an MBA from IMD Lausanne, a Doctorate of Sciences from the University of Geneva, a 3rd cycle Doctorate from the University of Strasbourg, and a Chemist Engineer Diploma from the Mulhouse National Superior School

(ENSCMu) and to explore various fields of creativity (news publication, tango compositions, Chinese ink drawing expositions). After eight years of research in theoretical particle physics, during which time paper, pencils and erasers were my main partners, I needed to open myself up to others and establish relationships that would allow me to share and collaborate with people from other backgrounds. So I decided to leave research to become… a salesperson. Many people asked me the question, sometimes with a little smile: "How can a researcher become a salesperson?" In general I answered "Just a lucky break!" To answer the question more seriously, I allow myself a small digression. I have always considered that *the essence of the human spirit is to find non-trivial links between trivial things*.

For example, take a series of little black circles. What could be more trivial? Arrange them on a sheet of music in a certain order and you get Beethoven's *Sonata Pathétique* or Erroll Garner's *Misty*. In fact, in any field, there is a way to *discover* hidden correlations, underlying processes, and subtle, non-trivial links, between objects, representations and behaviors that are quite ordinary and trivial.

Sales is no exception. On one side there are needs, often known but sometimes not perceived or expressed. On the other side, there are solutions, often standard but sometimes not adjusted, or complete. The art of the salesperson consists of listening to one and adopting the other to align the sales offer with the request. It is always about relationships and exchange.

In 1985, I joined **IBM**, an exceptional company that gave me the opportunity to learn sales from A to Z, to lead sales teams in different sectors, to direct one of its subsidiaries, CGI Switzerland, then the European marketing department for its semiconductor division, and finally, to direct business relations with some of our largest Swiss customers.

When you want to move ahead in a large group, sooner or later the time comes to make a crucial choice: what place in my life will I accept to give to my career? And the question *Why?* becomes more and more pressing and intense. What meaning am I going to give to what I am doing, to my choices, to who I am… what is power?… what does it mean to be rich?… what is leadership?… what does it mean to be a manager?… a director?… a spouse?… a parent?…

The mentoring system is well-developed at IBM. Several mentors helped me answer my questions and made me more attentive to certain career choices, which gave me the opportunity to practice several professions under the same umbrella and gave meaning to my choices. I have always needed to make sense of what I am doing and I wanted to pass this on to my daughters, to share it with my teams, and to apply it to my relationships with my customers. But mentoring has its limits, so I decided to begin taking coaching training. Which is how, for the last twelve years, coaching progressively entered into my professional activity and expanded to coaching directors and external sales teams.

Life has provided me with a lot of happiness and I have been fortunate, certainly thanks to my own resources but above all to alliances with others, to always doing what I like. It is now time to share what life has given me.

I hope you enjoy the book!

WHY DID I WRITE THIS BOOK?

Sales is an extraordinary profession. Yet how many parents dream of their child becoming a salesperson? What did your parents say when you chose this profession? Did you really choose it? Or did you rather adopt it by default? How do you feel doing it? Are you proud? If, like the majority of salespeople, you answered these questions negatively, this book is for you.

In many Western countries, salespeople don't like to be called salespeople. In France, the country of Descartes, salespeople are called Sales Engineers or Business Engineers, even if they went to a business school and did not study engineering. In English-speaking countries, where the manager is king, salespeople in industrial companies are called Key Account Managers, and those in the banking sector prefer the title Client Relationship Manager.

They believe it looks better on a business card and it seems to flatter their ego. Many salespeople say "they are in business", or they "do business"; it is rare that they say they are "a salesperson".

This lack of respect for sales comes from the fact that this profession is perceived to be easy and doesn't necessarily require a diploma. It is associated with money and the lure of profit, and, too often, the buyer's feeling of "being had".

It's true that this profession does not necessarily require a diploma. However, if it takes five years on average to educate an engineer, a doctor or a lawyer, it takes five years to educate a salesperson. As we will see, this education is not based on long academic training and the essentials are learned in the field, but it does require qualities, skills and distinct knowledge that take time to acquire, develop, and mature.

My first motivation for writing this book is to give those that practice this profession reasons to be proud, to dream and to achieve their dreams. Sales is a magnificent profession because it is based on what we have been doing since we were children, and since man has existed: exchange.

Sales is an exchange, monetized yes, but above all, an exchange. Like all exchanges, it is satisfying only if each party has the feeling that they have received what was expected for what was given. This satisfaction is based largely on emotional and behavioral factors that are not taught in a traditional academic curriculum, and which are sorely lacking. Indeed, engineers must know and master these factors in order to have their ideas adopted and doctors must integrate them into their practices if they want to move out of their strict role of "diagnosing illnesses". Recognizing our emotions, adopting behavior that will optimize the satisfaction of the two parties, is not natural or easy, and cannot be improvized. For the salesperson, it is essential.

My second motivation comes from the observation that, more and more, we are moving toward a sales style that is essentially transactional, at the expense of relational sales. This imbalance results from, on one hand, a demand for increasing efficiency to satisfy our company's financial return requirements, and on the other hand, from the acceleration of the commercialization processes due to the increasing speed of technology.

The order "here and now", leitmotiv of "short-termism" is widespread, and the search for quick gain, exacerbated by the examples of a few successful start-ups, pushes us to always go faster. The breaking up of sales activities into a series of anonymized processes, as required and popularized by "online sales", applies more and more to activities related to human interaction. Even so, we forget that an online sale is actually more of a purchase than a sale. Despite its subtle marketing techniques, by definition, it is not Amazon that sells me a book. It is me that buys a book from Amazon. Yet, the real sale begins when your client tells you "no"! It is at this moment that your role becomes noble and your profession as a salesperson takes on all its meaning. This observation led me to reflect and to use tools with success and passion for thirty years and to share them with sales teams and have them validated by clients. The positive feedback ended up convincing me to write this book, which addresses, above all, salespeople with three to five years of experience and recently promoted sales managers.

What is this book about?

Each one of our activities stems from our knowledge (*savoir*), our know-how (*savoir-faire*) and our human skills (*savoir-être*), illustrated in the pyramid below. While these three levels are all connected to our mindset, emotions and behavior, it is our knowledge that favors our intellect, our know-how that is reflected in our behavior, and our human skills that are rooted in our innermost emotions.

While knowledge can be gained in a few days or weeks and know-how requires several months or years to master, human skills (our capacity to behave appropriately in any situation and use emotional information to guide thinking and behavior) require decades to develop. Most sales books offer valuable advice and techniques about sales knowledge and know-how. This book focuses instead on know-how and human skills that will set you apart by making you a salesperson that knows why you chose to be one; is happy to be one; is appreciated by your clients and your peers; knows how to develop your empathy, your humility, your sincerity and your leadership; knows how to take care of your body, your mind and your emotions; and is able to integrate your profession into a harmonious life in which *you* have decided what is the most important.

This book focuses on personality rather than knowledge. It aims to be, first and foremost, a sharing of practical experience. It is intended for salespeople or sales managers that are new to the profession and have the three to five years of experience necessary to be able to ask the right questions. It will also be of interest to those looking to advance in sales by working on themselves. This work requires discipline, perseverance and humility. It requires discipline, because sales requires a commitment to rigor, often misunderstood or ignored, but which pays off in the long-term. For example: "say what you do and do what you say" is proof of commitment whose daily practice increases your credibility.

It requires perseverance, to overcome the many obstacles that can arise with your client, within your company and in your head. A purchase is, above all, a source of change for your client and all change requires time to get used to, either for your client, for their team or their company. Mobilizing the resources of your company and motivating your teams to overcome the growing bureaucracy of processes requires perseverance. As we will see, sales is a science, an art and a state of mind. Your mindset is essential to be able to apply yourself, to not give up, to know how to let go in order to bounce back better and to let time take care of its work. Transactional sales target the short-term. Relational sales feed on the long-term.

Humility is required to be able to recognize that your client always is "right", regardless of whether they are actually right or wrong on this or that technical, financial or strategic point. Clients are the final arbiters of their choices and so they have their reasons. This is not to say that you are wrong. Sales is not confrontation. There is not a winner and a loser. One of the key assumptions of this book is that clients know their needs and the solutions to meet those needs. Your role as a salesperson is to guide the client and help them recognize their needs and bring out the best solution. It is not up to you to put yourself in the client's place saying: "if I were in your position, here is what I would do", but to help the client by telling yourself "if I was the client, what could I do?" That is the nature of empathy. For this, you need to let yourself go and enter into the client's mental and emotional universe, to understand and to accept their point of view, to listen to what they say and to what they do not say. From that point on, it is up to you to guide the client by bringing forth the added value of your own products and/or services and in building together, with the client's skills and resources, what makes sense for their business. To summarize my deepest belief: "Selling is coaching your client".

How should you read this book?

The methods and techniques that I refer to are not my own and I am not promoting them in particular. I practiced them all and use them regularly, even daily. They suit me well and I have adapted some of them to my way of working. So I would like to share them with you as a testimonial.

To benefit from the advice and methods presented in this book, many of which are the product of the advancements in positive psychology and cognitive behavioral therapy that have taken place over the last decade, the only tool you need is yourself; whether it be your body, your mind or your emotions.

These advancements have helped people become more autonomous in their fulfillment by addressing the three centers of intelligence: physical, mental and emotional. The ideal is probably to read the book linearly, to be able to discover its main theme and underlying logic, even if you need to come back later to certain chapters as your profession deems, or if you would like to take a break and put things into perspective in terms of your own experience.

Chapter 1 addresses the importance of giving meaning to your life and the power that you have to decide. It helps you choose the type of life you would like to lead, in a world of uncertainty and imperfection, through a simple approach: Goal-Objectives-Projects-Actions.

Chapter 2 makes you think about the reasons why you chose to become a salesperson, or why you could become a sales manager. It makes you reflect on the type of sales, client, product and environment you prefer.

In Chapter 3, you will explore a series of steps that will allow you to excel. First, you will work with a very powerful tool, the personal SWOT, in order to identify your intrinsic Strengths, to use them to minimize your Weaknesses and external Threats, and to seize the numerous Opportunities that you will encounter. Then you will get acquainted with a psychodynamic personality model, the Enneagram, to discover how you function and to identify your underlying motivations. Finally, I will show you how healthy ambition, together with sincere humility, will make your life and career evolve toward the goals that you have set for yourself.

In Chapter 4 you will face the heart of sales, which is how to convince a client that tells you "no". The negotiation begins, in fact, when you say "hello" to your client. We will see how to build a relationship of confidence, starting with your first meeting, based on authenticity, respect and empathy. A real life story will illustrate how these three qualities are at the heart of all successful customer experiences. Then we will study how to co-develop a partnership over the long-term by building a strategy with your client that targets the short, medium and long-term. Although these three horizons have different time frames, you must develop them concurrently and start doing so now.

We will address the need to identify sponsors within your client's organization, as well as those who "make" the decisions and those who "take" the decisions. This distinction is fundamental to successfully conclude a sale. A successful negotiation is based on three pillars: relationships, content and the communication process. You will see why it's important to agree on the process right from the start. Finally, a stratagem, borrowed from Churchill, will show you to what extent silence is golden in order to win a sale.

Chapter 5 explores why and how to coach your client. In general, clients know most of their needs. We will see how, by relying on the alliance that you establish with them and with a humble inquiry approach, you will help your client to express their needs and come up with new options that they hadn't necessarily thought of before. All acts of purchase represent a change for your client whether it be on an individual basis, for their team or their company. We will see how the motivational interview, drawn from the medical world, is a powerful stimulant for your client to accept and appropriate this change, which is a precondition for them to buy.

In Chapter 6 you will deal with the essence of your leadership in depth and how to best use the available resources from your business ecosystem for the benefit of the partnership with your client. You will see how to lead a Jazz Team, find your mentors, take care of your communication, allow yourself to be helped and to intelligently handle your management.

Chapter 7 gives you advice on taking care of yourself, centered on three types of "hygiene": physical, mental and emotional. We all know that you need to sleep well, eat well and practice a physical activity to stay in good shape.

We will see how to optimize these three areas, but this is not enough. Mindfulness meditation, exercises from positive psychology, Marshall Rosenberg's non-violent communication, the Emotional Freedom Techniques of Gary Craig, or cardiac coherence are a few practices that will allow you to gain clarity, serenity, kindness and confidence in yourself, all while managing your daily stress.

Chapter 8 helps you to focus on what you have decided are the most important things in your life. You will see that it is healthier and enjoyable to do less, in order to succeed more.

Each chapter ends with a brief summary of the points to remember, including some exercises to put into practice, according to your needs and your experience.

CHAPTER 1

YOUR LIFE IS NOT A REHEARSAL

Life's only meaning is the meaning that we give it. I know this point of view is debatable, but it guides my life.

It began to take shape for me when I was a young physicist. While physics helped me understand how things work by explaining the chain of underlying mechanisms, it wasn't able to provide me with the objective, the purpose or the meaning. Not drawn to the idea of designating this capacity to an external entity, which would only put off the question on a larger scale, I became convinced that there wasn't, in principle, a meaning, to the world around us. Therefore, if I wanted and needed the meaning for my own existence, my actions, and my choices, I had to give it to myself. This belief is embedded in the works of Viktor Frankl, an exceptional man who made the choice in 1945, when he was a prisoner at the Auschwitz camp, to continue to live to "help others each find a meaning to their life" (Frankl, 2000, 2004, 2014).

It then became a reality throughout the rest of my life. I noticed that those that shared the same belief had a life that was rich, full, proactive and authentic, because this point of view is based on two fundamental pillars: freedom, and the responsibility that comes from it. By that I mean, your freedom to decide what you would like to do with your life and how you would like to live it. Your freedom to decide what you would like to achieve and how you would like to achieve it. Your freedom to decide who you would like to share your life with. Your freedom to choose your profession, where or how you are going to work. Your freedom to choose the country that you live in.

Of course, you are born, grow up, and develop with certain physical, religious or social constraints. Nevertheless, you have the freedom to overcome these constraints, to refuse them or to accept them.

Your freedom implies responsibility: you are accountable for the choices that you make, the actions that result from them and the consequences. Your responsibility is the price to pay for your freedom. As the Swiss priest and writer Joël Pralong quite rightly says: "You are not responsible for who you are, but for who you become".

Give meaning to your life

Giving meaning to your life helps you define how you would like to live it. The word "meaning" can be interpreted in two ways: significance and direction. To be in harmony with the objective that you set for yourself, the steps that will bring you there and the means that you give yourself, is a key factor in your fulfillment. Defining your life course calls for setting goals and the way to reach them. Neuroscience explains that when we set goals we are happier and we achieve more than if we hadn't. This takes place in our brain. Achieving a goal produces dopamine, a powerful neurotransmitter responsible for the feeling of pleasure. And reciprocally, dopamine activates the neural circuits that drive you to pursue new challenges.

There are many ways to give meaning to your life and they all focus on thinking, feeling, doing, or a mix of the three. You can find meaning through your own reflection, taking lessons from the past, identifying a mission for yourself or by developing your life plan. You can also experience an emotion or a feeling that resonates deeply within you, to the point of feeling a conviction that you cannot explain, but which is so present that the meaning of your life naturally flows from it.

Finally, some of us find the meaning through daily actions. If this is your case, you are building your life day after day, stone by stone, knowing that you are part of something big. "Giving meaning to one's life" reminds me of the story of three stonemasons that are asked what they are doing. The first one answers: "I am earning my living". The second one answers: "I am building a wall". And the third one exclaims: "I am building a cathedral". Whether you are the architect or the stonemason doesn't matter. What matters, is that it is up to you to give meaning to your life, because no one will do it in your place.

Giving meaning to your life does not mean that it is set forever. As life moves on, you accumulate the experiences, discoveries and encounters that will enrich, perfect and modify the deep meaning that you give to your life.

These same experiences, discoveries and encounters will offer you, in many cases, the opportunity to change the direction that was initially planned. Sometimes, the hazards and circumstances of life oblige you to change, even if it's not what you would like. In both cases, deliberately chosen or not, this change in direction modifies, at times profoundly, the meaning that you give to your life. It is up to you to keep control and steer this change toward a new course whose purpose you have chosen. The meaning that you give to your life will nourish it. At the same time, your life will nourish the meaning that you have given it.

Uncertainty is everywhere

No matter which field we look at, whether it be health, politics, ecology, finance, social life, technology or science, uncertainty reigns everywhere. The latest advances in artificial intelligence attempt to minimize this uncertainty by inferring predictions from the past, establishing links and identifying hidden patterns within huge reservoirs of more or less precise data. But uncertainty, largely the outcome of the world's growing complexity, is also due to human behavior, dictated by emotions and ego. Emotions and ego are the source of sudden and unforeseeable decisions and actions, capable of destroying in a few hours or days, the most beautiful technical, architectural, intellectual, political, social or environmental structures, patiently built over several years, decades, or even centuries.

Imperfection is the rule

We all try to make perfect choices. Not necessarily perfect in absolute terms, but in our eyes. Choosing the best partner, the best job, giving the best education to our children, purchasing the house of our dreams, taking the best holidays, etc. However, it doesn't always work, simply because perfection doesn't exist. On one hand, what may be the best at a given time, is not necessarily a few years later. On the other hand, we can't control the way that our choices unfold, because of the previously mentioned uncertainty. In addition, we have to take into account our own imperfection, which implies that we make more mistakes than we would care to.

Learn from falling

You must learn to live with these two elements of reality – uncertainty and imperfection, and accept them as facts of life, so that you can fall on your feet in the event of hardship; accept them as a source of humility in order to overcome your frustrations and mistakes; and embrace them and transform them into strength and success. Like many of us, I had such an experience with the stock exchange. There's nothing more uncertain than financial markets, and nothing more imperfect than how we function when spurred on by fear or greed. After the technology bubble burst in 2000, I found myself financially "knocked out" and frustrated by my arrogance at believing that I could control the market. It took me a few years to pick myself back up, during which time I learned from professionals how to understand the market, structure a strategy for allocating assets, minimize risk – but not cancel it – thanks to rigorous management of market positions (money management) and by putting my emotions aside and working with a trading plan that is almost algorithmic.

Learning to relate to money is full of valuable lessons. The experience taught me a lot about my beliefs and my emotions, but it also taught me, above all, to face risks, accept patience and to let go. This has allowed me, for the last few years, to manage a portion of my assets myself with a satisfactory return, while letting the experts take care of what I don't know how to.

Thus, failure is not in falling, it is in not getting up. A child who is learning to walk, falls; that's normal, it is not a situation of weakness or failure. The child learns, as we all learn from falling; from higher or lower heights, with more or less damage, and more or less pain. Again, it is not a failure; it's the normal process of learning what life is about. Failure is staying stuck at the bottom. It is wallowing in a dependence on discomfort that we accept, despite the suffering it may cause.

Of course, this doesn't mean that getting back up is quick or easy to do. At times, life is not at all the same after a fall. But we always have the choice to get back up. It is one of the qualities of human beings.

So it is one of your qualities. It is up to you to steer your life through this prevailing uncertainty, despite your imperfection and that of the world around you, regardless of the injuries and accidents along the way.

Choose your life

This steering takes place, on one hand, through a variety of small daily choices, and on the other, through a certain number of key decisions, which only happen a few times in your life. These are the ones that you must take special care of because they are vital in that their impact will unfold over the course of several years or decades. Like in ballistics, the starting angle is crucial to reach the greatest heights and achieve the longest distance. Once your key choice has been made and implemented – for example your choice of partner, profession, whether to have children, the country that you will settle in – it will not be easy to change it. Not impossible (with the exception of the decision to have children) but not easy.

Choosing is to renounce. It's the opening of one door and closing of others, sometimes for a long time. This is why it is essential that you know the *Why?* and the *What for?* of your choice, as I do for the country where I live. Switzerland is a country that I like, one that welcomed me to pursue my doctorate, offered me the possibility to work, and where my daughters were born. I like its very democratic nature, which is shaped directly by its people through a system of referendums that allows them to express themselves several times a year on all the subjects that affect citizens. The subjects range from increasing taxes to the purchase of fighter planes by the army, to limiting bonuses for senior managers. I'm comfortable with this efficient way of operating that makes the people entirely responsible for the choices they make. I appreciate its economy, which is both liberal and pragmatic. Lastly, I like the diversity of its population, a quarter of which are foreigners, and whose inventiveness earns its ranking as the country with the second highest level of patents per inhabitant after Japan.

So, I wanted to become Swiss, and to become Swiss, you must really want to. At the time, you had to have lived in Switzerland for twelve years and then wait another two years during the naturalization process, without having left the territory for more than one year during this entire period. Otherwise, you had to start all over again. This choice to live in accordance with certain deep values thus led me to close certain doors in terms of career development abroad.

Your Life Apartment

In this context, here is a first question that I invite you to reflect upon: What type of life do you want to live?

A metaphor can help you to reply: imagine that your life is a big apartment, and each room corresponds to an important part of it: for example, your family, your profession, your relationships or hobbies. Imagine also that the size of each room is proportional to the importance that you give to each part of your life. Do you prefer a big professional living room, with a small kitchen and a small master bedroom? Or rather a small office next to a comfortable family room and a big sports room? As you can see, there are many possibilities. It is up to you to give your Life Apartment the shape that you would like, and the size and number of rooms that you wish. This layout should be based on free choice and fully thought through.

On one hand, this approach will help you determine the importance of the meaning you have given to each element. By giving a meaning to each part, you will find a more complete meaning overall.

On the other hand, it will allow you to define how you would like to manage your time. What do you want to spend your time on? With whom? How much time would you like to dedicate to your family, to your profession, to your health and your wellbeing? The bigger the room is, the more important it is and you spend more time there.

Like for any choice, nothing is permanent. You can use movable walls. This allows you to start with a certain configuration and then, little by little, when your career develops, your family grows and your responsibilities expand, you can reconsider the size and even the number of rooms in your life apartment.

A little word of warning: when one of the rooms is disproportionately large compared to the others, in the case of a flood, the entire apartment is ruined. That being said, there is no good or bad architecture for the life apartment. It all depends on what you want to do. What is most important is that you enjoy living there, you know what is intended for each room and you can spend the amount of time you decided to in each room.

This image came to me following the death of my father a few days after his 60th birthday. I was 37. Coming from a very modest family, my father succeeded, thanks to his sharp intelligence and tireless work, in creating the South American subsidiaries of a large French group and then became responsible for the international division. That enabled him to climb the social ladder, pay for an education of our choosing and provide security for my mother. Nevertheless, I didn't see him take a holiday for thirty years. An accomplished pianist, curious about a number of subjects, he said that he would dedicate himself to his passions when he retired, which unfortunately he didn't have the time to do. At the time of his death, I realized that we saw each other one week per year over twenty years. While I consoled myself by thinking that he lived the life that he had chosen, I wondered about the balance of his choice.

A few years later, this questioning led me to refuse a promotion to the USA. I had just separated, my daughters were young teenagers and I didn't want them to have the same experience that I had with my own father, only seeing each other a few weeks each year. I had to face the questions: what does it mean to be a father? What meaning should I give to my own fatherhood? I answered these questions by telling them that, on one hand I was a guide, a bit like a travel guide, that they could question, listen to, then decide to follow or not the advice provided. And on the other hand, I was a home port, and whatever happened, they could always come home, come back, before leaving again. This decision, this choice, allowed us, among other things, to develop the bond that we have today. It is one of the best choices that I ever made. It made me rearrange my Life Apartment by reducing the size of the office to increase the size of the family room.

How to furnish your Life Apartment

The second question for you to reflect upon is about your life objectives: What would you like to accomplish in each of the rooms of your Life Apartment?

Only you can provide the answer, and the following approach can help you find it. It is inspired by some excellent advice from Peter Bregman (2012).

First of all, formulate a goal for each part of your life. For the moment, it is not a matter of formulating a precise and detailed objective, but an overall goal expressed openly. For example, it could be: "Take care of my family" or "Ensure the education of my children" in the family environment, "Direct the sales division for Asia within three years" or "Be my own boss before the age of thirty" in the professional environment, "Run a marathon in the next 24 months" or "Earn a doctorate in positive psychology" in the personal area. Having four or five directions, sufficiently defined, without being too rigid, brings you clarity and serenity. Then, for each of these goals, list the objectives for the year that will help reach them. It is not worth listing too many. Three annual objectives per goal is more than enough. For example: "Exceed my annual sales objectives", "Educate myself" and "Find a mentor within upper management" to prepare your promotion to Asia. Then identify projects whose results are key to reach each objective. These projects can require one to six months, depending on the nature of the objective. For example, it is essential to achieve your quarterly, and even monthly results, depending on the type of industry you are working in, if you want to exceed your annual objectives. Learning basic Chinese will require several years, while identifying a mentor could only take a few days and their support will only require a few hours per year. Lastly, for each of these projects, list the actions that you will take each week or each day.

The GOPA tree

The best way to memorize this approach is to associate a GOPA tree to each room in your life apartment. The trunk is your Goal, the boughs are your Objectives, the branches form your Projects – the twigs of the branches would be sub-projects – and the leaves are the Actions that you assign yourself and which should be updated regularly. Four levels, G-O-P-A, are easy to remember and visualize and will enable you to start from an essential goal and move on to the details of its implementation in each area of your life.

The GOPA Tree

The first step

However, all of this is not enough to advance. The essential and indispensable step to really give meaning to your life and to transform this meaning into reality, is to *take the first step*. It is both simple and difficult, and nothing will be done without it. After you have made your life a dream, it will allow you to make the dream a reality, as Little Prince of Antoine of Saint Exupéry would have said.

Once you have started, the most efficient way to reach all your objectives is to be highly focused on concentrating all of your efforts on a target objective. This concentration brings together your ideas, makes you creative, and simultaneously stimulates your physical, intellectual and emotional capacities. It boosts your actions by avoiding duplication, loss of time and other unnecessary setbacks. Focusing does not mean that you should only do one thing, or only pursue one objective. It means that you should concentrate on *one thing at a time* and allow the time necessary to achieve it. By having defined the essential areas of your life and focusing your efforts on the goals, the objectives, the projects and the actions related to them, your life will be led in an optimal, efficient, harmonious and serene way.

Key take-aways

- Decide the meaning you want to give to your life

- Use the freedom this meaning gives you

- Assume the responsibilities that come from this freedom

- Draw your Life Apartment

- Determine a goal for each room

- Set objectives, projects and actions, for each goal

- Take the first step

- Only focus on the essential

- Accept that you may fall… and then get back up

CHAPTER 2

KNOW WHY YOU ARE A SALESPERSON

Why did you become a salesperson? Is it by chance? Because you don't have a diploma? Or by choice? The first two answers are not the best. From experience, only the third one makes sense if you want to become an excellent salesperson.

Sales is a valid profession. It takes about five years to educate an engineer, a doctor or a lawyer, and it takes about five years to become a professional salesperson.

Sales is, above all, a state of mind that requires discipline, self-confidence, is based on technical and relational skills, and requires psychological tools. As a consequence, sales is at the same time, a state of mind, an art and a science.

Unlike more academic professions, whose education takes place mainly on auditorium seats, that of a salesperson takes place 80% in the field and 20% in class. However, the amount of time necessary to acquire a solid base and professional assurance is about the same, and we must not forget that it's not because fewer hours are spent in class compared to the number of hours spent in the field, that the sales profession is less intelligent than engineering, more mundane than law or more trivial than medicine. This is because for sales people, their *savoir-être* (personality) plus their *savoir-faire* (behavior) outweighs the importance of their *savoir* (knowledge). The sales people that succeed have well developed emotional and relational intelligence, which complement their intellectual intelligence, thus combining a wide range of analytical, logical, intuitive and human skills.

Having practiced other professions, I can tell you that the sales profession is as passionate as research or teaching. In fact, like all professions, it is magnificent from the moment that you feel comfortable in it and you succeed. It is therefore important that you understand your deepest motivations for becoming a salesperson. It will help you set up your Life Apartment that we spoke about in the preceding chapter, give you a goal and, in the end, give meaning to your professional life. Don't let anyone else but you, and least of all chance, make the choice of embracing this magnificent profession.

What is your push–pull?

If you want to know why to become a salesperson, or why to remain one and how to advance, use the push–pull approach. In any choice, there is a push side and a pull side. The push side makes us run from what we don't like. The pull side makes us go toward what we like.

For example, your push side could come from what you don't like:

- Having a routine activity.

- Being closed in an office all day long.

- Being limited financially.

- Having a fixed salary that is not linked to your results.

- Depending on fixed hours.

- Being in contact with a limited number of people.

- …

These reasons are not bad in and of themselves. They are even very valued, and sought after by certain professions, whether it be for security reasons, simplicity of operation, minimization of risks, or purely taste. However, if they are not what you are looking for, it's important that you are aware.

At the same time, it is important that you know your pull side, which is based on the fact that you like, for example:

- Interacting with a lot of people.

- Working in different cultures (industrial sectors, countries…)

- Negotiating.

- Gaining recognition quickly.

- Having objectives.

- Succeeding.

- Being in the heat of the action.

- Managing; being in control.

- Working in teams.

- Being paid based on your results.

- Earning a lot of money.

- ...

Be careful, the financial reason should be taken with a grain of salt because "a lot" doesn't mean anything. It is subjective and depends on who it is coming from. Some consider $100,000 to be a lot, others aim for at least $1,000,000, others set the threshold at $10,000,000 and some aim even higher. It is up to you. It depends on your mindset, the price that you are prepared to pay and the risks that you are ready to take to earn a lot of money. It also depends on your answer to the question: "For what?"

The size of the room that you allocate to your profession in your Life Apartment will depend on your answer, and therefore the size of the other rooms as well...

What type of sales do you prefer?

Once you have an idea about your motivations for becoming a real sales professional, it is important that you know which type of sales attracts you: tangible or intangible sales. Let me explain. In tangible sales, you are selling a concrete product that the client can touch, turn on, make work or use as a service (for example, a car, software program or insurance contract). The majority of the profession is in tangible sales.

While intangible sales involve, above all, selling confidence in one's company and taking responsibility for the relationship between the company and the client. This type of salesperson operates on another level, establishing a strong relationship with the client in order to understand their needs, then to direct a team of specialists that will design and sell the solution to meet these needs. This is what I call intangible sales even if, ultimately, the client obtains and pays for something tangible. This approach is common in many industries (wealth management, IT, aerospace, nuclear…) and in the large companies that represent these sectors.

As we are going to see in more detail, these two practices require certain types of profiles, education, and experience. This being said, there are three questions that you can ask yourself:

1. What type of people do you like to do business with?

2. Which type of product are you the most comfortable with?

3. What kind of environment do you like working in?

Let's take these questions one at a time, because they are fundamental for you to be truly efficient, successful and happy in your job.

What type of client do you prefer?

Above all, it is crucial that you know who you like to interact with, especially if you are in intangible sales. This will allow you to not only be at ease, but to also quickly develop an alliance with your client. Because if you "like them," they will "like you" back. It is the famous "action-reaction" principle applied to sales. This tendency to go toward others must be natural and really genuine on your part for the alliance to work. If you force yourself, your contact will feel it, become suspicious, or even close off to all exchange. So you must show a real interest in your client and a pleasure in being interested in them, their environment and issues.

This alliance is based on three essential relational qualities: kindness, empathy and sincerity.

Who do you feel comfortable with? Which environment interests you? Engineering, artistic, financial, civil service, medical, social work?

Are you at ease among people who are rich, influential and powerful? How do you feel about money, hierarchy, or politics? Fascination, envy, embarrassment, comfort, complicity? Are you at ease with laborers, technicians and contacts more oriented to concrete achievement than global concepts?

Do you prefer to be in contact with people that are analytical and rigorous, or more emotional and creative?

How do you behave in front of a company head? With other members of the management team? Do you prefer contact with the management of human resources, research and development, finance, marketing? Or with purchasing management – which would be unusual for a salesperson!

These questions inevitably bring you back to yourself. Are you the instinctive, emotional or mental type? Very optimistic, optimistic or realistic? It is out of the question that you are pessimist, that wouldn't be very salesperson-like…

Are you comfortable with your emotions? Can you recognize, express and control them? Sales is essentially based on emotions. Even to sell one of the most powerful computers in the world, as a long-time colleague and friend of mine succeeded in doing, he had to understand the emotions, the sensibilities and the needs of their client, of the client's team and colleagues, as well as their own.

As you can see, there are many different types of clients. Which is what makes this profession exciting and full of many diverse encounters.

What type of product do you prefer?

The ideal, if you practice tangible sales, is to sell products that you are passionate about. One day, one of my staff told me that he was leaving his job because he had been offered a position as product manager at one of the best watch manufacturers in Switzerland. I was curious to learn about his motivations for moving from IT to luxury watches. He admitted that he had been a watch collector since his adolescence, that he was passionate about the concentration of creativity in the high precision engineering of our beautiful Geneva and Jura watches, and that he had the chance to be able to play an active role in his passion. Despite my frustration at losing an excellent salesperson, I was really happy for him, because he had found his calling.

Without passion, we won't go anywhere. However, not everyone necessarily has a passion, you are going to say. This is true, but if you accept the basic principle that the meaning of life is what you decide it to be, then the passion will come along the way, as you integrate this meaning into each act of your life. On one condition: that you do it well. Whatever you do, do it all the way and do it well. There is a natural, involuntary and automatic strengthening that takes place when we do things thoroughly and correctly. It awakens a pleasure: the enjoyment of having transformed what had been just an idea, a concept or a word, into an object, a painting, a book… or a contract, the product of hundreds of hours of work and negotiations.

We could summarize these ideas in two principles:

"Like what you do and do what you like" and

"Master what you do and do what you master".

Life, therefore, becomes easier.

The range of products and services is infinite. Do you prefer high-tech products, works of art, financial products, or health-related products? Everyday consumer products or sophisticated products?

For example, in finance, selling a structured product requires an interest in mathematics and abstraction to be able to explain to the client the evolution mechanisms of the various product elements according to the market.

In the automobile industry, an interest in design, user friendliness and mechanics will allow you to better understand the emotions of your client and to answer in an appropriate way.

What kind of environment do you prefer?

Finally, what kind of environment do you like to work in? Ranging from the size of the company to the style of management. Even if sales in a start-up follows certain basic rules that are identical to sales in a multinational, the two environments operate in different ways. Each one has distinctive constraints and opportunities, and is fuelled by different types of relational interaction, depending on the degree of hierarchical formalities.

It is therefore essential to know where you feel at ease. It's a question of common sense. But I have seen this common sense forgotten at times and the realization is rough when there is a difference between what is asked of you and what you like to give. For example, the dynamics and success of a trendy start-up can make us forget our need for structure. Or the prestige of a multinational can temporarily wash away our need for autonomy and quick decision-making.

There are no good or bad answers to these questions. There are only answers that are more or less adapted to your personality and to the personality of the people you like to work with, whether it be your clients, your colleagues or your hierarchy; to your tastes and passions; and to the type of organizations you like to work in, whether it be that of your clients' or your company.

Knowing why you have become a salesperson is therefore essential, not only to feel good about yourself, in your daily professional practice and in your relationships with your family and friends, but also to become even better, no matter what your current performance level is.

Key take-aways

- What is your push, what is your pull?

- Define your type of client

- Define your type of product

- Define your preferred type of environment

- Like what you do and do what you like

- Master what you do and do what you master

CHAPTER 3

YOU ARE GOOD, NOW BECOME GREAT

If you are reading this book it is because you have the drive to develop yourself, to improve yourself and to become even better in your profession as a salesperson. We are all good in several areas and not as good in others. It is up to you to identify those areas in which you are good, in order to become excellent.

To begin, here is a list of skills and qualities necessary for sales that you could recognize in yourself and nurture daily. I selected them from the Strengths Cards by Dr. Ilona Boniwell a specialist in positive psychology.

Action oriented	Active listening
Adaptability	Appreciation
Bravery	Communication
Competition	Confidence
Creativity	Curiosity
Education	Empathy
Improvement	Integrity
Humility	Humor
Kindness	Leadership
Loyalty	Motivation

Optimism	Open-mindedness
Persuasion	Planning
Resiliency	Responsibility
Self-awareness	Self-control
Self-discipline	Seduction
Sociability	Solution oriented
Strategic	Time management
Teamwork	Vitality

It's essential that you know what you are good at. This will guide you toward the types of relationships in which you will feel at ease, the types of products that you will like to sell and the types of environments in which you will enjoy working. Knowing your strengths helps you gain confidence in yourself, develop it in others and recover yourself in the event of failure.

For example, one of my strengths is to inspire confidence. I have had this strength since I was a child. I noticed very early on that when I said something, people listened to me and believed me. This led me to become aware of the responsibility I had when I spoke, and then to reflect and come to the conclusion to be sincere.

I certainly am not always right. However, when I state something, I believe what I say, and if I don't know, or I am not in agreement, I say that as well. This quality was partly innate for me and helped me a lot in my responsibilities as a salesperson, manager and coach. From the moment that I became aware of its importance, I wanted to strengthen it by developing two other skills: active listening and empathy.

Active listening consists of "fully" listening to others, by paying attention to both the form and the substance of what they express, either verbally or non-verbally; by "listening" to their silence, the density and duration; by "reading" in their eyes, the windows to the soul, the emotions that they are feeling at that moment.

Contrary to what one often hears, empathy is not saying to yourself: "What would I do in their place?" It is saying to yourself: "What would I do if I were them?" These two attitudes are fundamentally different. The first one looks at the other person's reality through your glasses and reaches conclusions that are shaped according to your vision of things. The second attitude goes into the other person's way of thinking, feeling and behaving by putting on their glasses. It leads you to conclusions that are shaped by their vision.

The result is a strong and close link, based on a deep and sincere understanding of your intermediary. Empathy is a quality essential to succeeding in sales. It is not necessarily innate. As we will see in Chapter 4, it is a skill that one can learn and develop.

To understand what makes you strong in a particular area, it's useful to step back and observe yourself: how do you succeed? Which aspects of your personality drive your actions? How do you feel when you take these actions? How do you know that you are doing the right thing? How do you measure your success?

The answers to these questions are precious. They will help you apply your own process for success to other areas in which you would like to improve. By knowing how to have muscular arms, you will know how to develop muscular legs. By understanding how you resolved a relationship problem with a colleague, you will improve your relationship with your children. Or vice-versa. By analyzing how you get out of a difficult situation, you will develop your capacity for resiliency.

What is your SWOT?

A good way to improve yourself is to conduct your own SWOT analysis, the acronym for Strengths, Weaknesses, Opportunities, and Threats. To do so, you identify, on one hand, your strengths and your inherent weaknesses, and on the other, the threats and external opportunities that come from your ecosystem.

This exercise, widely used in companies to analyze the strengths, weaknesses, threats and opportunities of either the company overall, a department or a project, can also be applied to yourself. It is extremely efficient and simple to implement. You just need to do it, in one sitting, in a calm place. You need a pencil, a piece of paper, and your head.

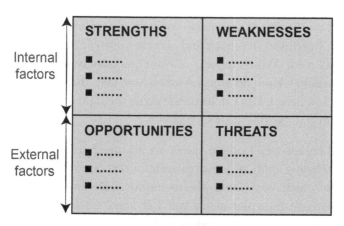

S.W.O.T.

Divide the paper into four numbered quadrants and list

1. Your strengths:

In addition to your human qualities that you pointed out in the preceding reflection, identify and add for example:

- Your capacity to work hard.

- Your specific technical skills (analytical, financial…).

- Your pleasant appearance.

- Your good health.

- Your friendly smile.

- Your desire to move about, to relocate, to experience other cultures.

- Your ambition and your desire to advance, to learn.

- …

2. Your weaknesses:

Identify the points to be improved that depend essentially on you, such as:

- Your limited technical knowledge (products, sectors…).

- Your lacking written, verbal or non-verbal communication skills.

- Your missing foreign language skills.

- Your addiction to the internet, to your smartphone, to the TV.

- Your extra weight.

- Your tendency to work too much.

- Your inertia to initiate things.

- Your professional overdependence on a product (which could become obsolete), a sector (which could be reduced), a profession (which could be relocated or disappear).

- ...

3. Your threats:

Identify the elements that could threaten your effective operation, your personal development or your career progression:

- A reorganization in your company.

- A change in legislation affecting your sector of activity.

- A competitive technology that could render your product obsolete.

- A difficult family situation.

- A limited personal and professional network.

- An undemanding professional environment.

- A deficient management hierarchy.

- …

4. Your opportunities:

Identify the elements that could contribute to your effective operation, your personal development or your career progression:

- A new education, a meditation or a fitness workshop.

- Available money (savings, bonus, inheritance).

- Developed personal and professional networks.

- Access to a mentor or a coach.

- An optimal family situation (young children allowing for greater mobility, an increase in revenue from your partner allowing you to expand your career choices…).

- An unexpected promotion.

- A strong dynamic in your industry or market.

- Expatriation possibilities proposed by your company.

- …

Coaching versus mentoring

It is useful to recall here the difference between your mentor and your coach.

Your mentor is someone with whom you have established a relationship of confidence, who knows you well, who has solid experience in your profession and your company, and who is able to guide you by telling you what would be best to do in this or that situation, how to avoid pitfalls, who to contact... In a way, your mentor guides you by telling you what they would do in your place, while taking into account your personality and your skills. A bit like the image of an experienced cabinetmaker who teaches their apprentice how to make a magnificent piece of furniture, all while taking into account the fact that the apprentice is, for example, left-handed.

Your coach is someone with whom you have established a relationship of confidence, who doesn't know you necessarily very well, who does not necessarily have experience in your profession or your company, and who is, at the same time, able to guide you by making you discover the strengths that are inside you and the resources you possess.

Confucius said: "When a man is hungry, it's better to teach him how to fish, than to give him a fish". In this spirit, a mentor will give you a fish to feed you and a coach will give you a fishing pole and teach you how to fish. Of course, it's not forbidden for your mentor to coach you, if they know how to do so.

How to use your SWOT

Once this work of reflection and writing has been accomplished, examine your strengths, understand how they function and how you can rely on and duplicate them in order to strengthen them and ensure their longevity. The ideal is to increase your reservoir of strengths as you gain experience. Each experience should reinforce one of these strengths or add a new one, day after day.

Following that, examine your weaknesses and make a plan to resolve them, either by using the mechanisms underlying your existing strengths, or by activating new repair mechanisms. This will contribute to you developing new strengths.

For example, in treating the insomnia that was starting to ruin my life, I became acquainted with cognitive-behavioral therapy (CBT) and I applied it to other areas to increase my wellbeing. I had already heard about CBT and the positive results that can be obtained for treating certain disorders. The success of using it to treat my insomnia opened me to a new field of interest for a discipline that is useful in my profession as a coach. I treated a weakness and gained new strengths that are not only useful in my personal life but also in my profession. We will look at these techniques in Chapter 7, which is devoted to taking care of yourself.

While it is relatively easy to identify our strengths and our weaknesses, it is more complicated to identify our threats. These do not depend on you as they come from your environment. They can be sudden (e.g. a drastic reorganization following the purchase of your company by a competitive group), progressive (e.g. the eruption of new technologies dethroning little by little your products and services), company internal (e.g. very "political" management and a poisonous ambiance), or your family situation.

Sometimes we are not aware of them, sometimes we deny them and put our head in the sand. It's advised to conduct a 360-degree analysis, as objectively as possible, of the current situation, then to measure progress regularly. This is what happens when we become an expert in a discipline, a product, a market or a profession. Comfortable with our expertise, after a personal investment of time, money and energy, things can change without us taking notice, or without us accepting to see these changes that take us out of our comfort zone. We have come full circle in our discipline and there is no more advancement possible. A competing technology can make our product obsolete in a few weeks. A specialized market can turn over in a few months. A profession can begin to relocate and become fragile in a few years. The risk is that you find yourself like the frog in a pan of cold water that is put on the stove. The water becomes warm and the frog feels good and sleepy; just until it is boiled alive. While this same frog, if thrown suddenly into boiling water would have jumped out of the pan and survived.

The difficulty in measuring our threats comes from the lack of hindsight. This hindsight can be brought by your mentor or coach, via a sabbatical period that takes you away from your daily routine, from a regular exchange with members of your network, and also from your own intuition. Listening to yourself, perceiving a problem that creeps in, a motivation that diminishes or a frustration that grows, allows you to react quickly and take the necessary corrective measures and jump out of the pan before you perish.

Opportunities are also not always obvious to see, easy to accept or to comprehend. Opportunity means change. Yet, all change implies a dose of uncertainty. And all change disrupts our comfort. Yet we don't like to leave our comfort, especially to go toward the unknown. So, even if it's to go toward something better, we risk missing an opportunity because of lack of foresight or courage. Which is why it is necessary to prepare ourselves to recognize these opportunities and to welcome them as such.

Determine your strengths and weaknesses clearly and calmly; look threats in the eye that are weighing on your professional future; identify and acquire new opportunities, such are the advantages of a structured approach like SWOT. It allows you to know where you are, where you want to go and can go, which pitfalls to avoid and to put together the basics of how to get there.

The Enneagram

In order to become even better than you are, it is essential that you know how you function. How do you behave when you let yourself go, when you are in your comfort zone? How do you act when you are stressed? What are you like when you are at the top of your form, both physical and mental? What are, in these three cases, your emotions and feelings: anger, frustration, impatience, fear, anxiety, sadness, nostalgia, joy, completeness, pride, strength? What are your methods of communication, the words and tone that you use, the look that you give others? Which ideas, images and mental associations, beliefs, automatic thoughts come to you…

One of the most powerful and most precious tools for assessing these elements and getting to know oneself deeply is the Enneagram. I discovered and learned about this approach ten years ago. Since then, I haven't stopped using it (with my family, my friends, my colleagues or my clients) and I find its value and depth each time I use it. The Enneagram is increasingly used in business leadership and executive coaching, and there are many useful writings about it (Anastaze, 2014; Lapid-Bogda, 2007; Madanes, 2011; Palmer, 1991, 1996; and many others). As a consequence, I will point out the basics, describe the advantages and benefits that one can gain and show how its use is powerful in sales.

First of all, the Enneagram is not an object or a software program that one buys. The Enneagram, whose name comes from the Greek and signifies nine points, is a personality psychodynamic model distributed around three centers (mental, instinctive, and emotional) and nine personality types describing nine different points of the view of life. As has been observed by numerous authors, notably Helen Palmer in the United States and Eric Salmon in France, we all use these nine points of view but the Enneagram postulates that we unconsciously favor one in particular. This is called our Enneatype, or more simply, "type". It originates from a dominant emotion that emerges during childhood like an adaptation strategy, and that leads us to adopt, as an adult, a behavior, associated with automatic thoughts and limiting beliefs. Graphically, the Enneagram is represented by a circle on which the nine enneatypes are arranged equidistantly and linked by a series of arrows according to a precise order and an underlying logic described later. For mnemonic reasons, numerous authors give each type the name of a character (i.e. Perfectionist, Altruist, Achiever, etc.) recalling its initial approach. Fortunately these names are similar between the different books about the Enneagram, which ensures consistency in reading. We will use the names the most often used, given by Helen Palmer. Nevertheless this glance must not hide the complexity of this typological approach, or introduce a limiting and distorted categorization of type.

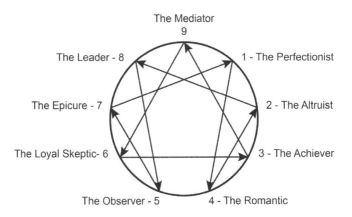

In a perspective of evolution, the dynamic model underlying the Enneagram thus connects our enneatype to four other types whose qualities and resources we can use to develop ourselves.

The four other types our enneatype is connected to are:

- the two adjacent types, called "wings"

- the "stress type" that is associated with it,

indicated by the exiting arrows

- the "serenity type" associated with it, indicated by the entering arrows.

When we are stressed, we adopt the behavior of our stress type. Whereas when we are serene, we adopt the behavior of our serenity type.

For example, my enneatype is the Achiever type (3). I have a tendency to be in the heat of the action, doing what it takes to achieve the results and thus satisfy my need for recognition. Sometimes I lean on my Altruistic wing (2), which is centered on generosity. Sometimes I adopt the sensitivity that is part of the Romantic (4). When I am very stressed, I have a tendency to procrastinate and seek refuge in the tardiness of the Mediator (9), whereas when I feel good, I use the doubt and questioning of the Loyal Skeptic (6) to dig deeper and advance. That does not mean that I become an Altruist (2), a Romantic (4), a Loyal Skeptic (6) or a Mediator (9). But I will adopt some of their traits, behaviors, peculiarities and qualities.

To use a metaphor, if our personality was a color, for example, red, certain "red" enneatypes would be really "bright red", others would be more orange, and others more mauve, because of the influence of their adjacent colors (i.e. their wings). Supposing that black is the stress type of red, it would go from "bright red" to "dark red". Supposing that white is the serenity type of red, the red would go from "bright red" to "light red".

Thus, two personalities with the same enneatype have similar motivations and behaviors but express them in a variety of ways.

What is your enneatype?

There are three ways to discover your type. The first is to answer a questionnaire on the internet. It's the easiest but it can be limited by the lack of objectivity inherent in all self-evaluations. The work of David Daniels and Virginia Price offers an excellent guide that uses a questionnaire-test validated by a statistical approach that was the subject of seven years of research with more than 900 Anglophones (Daniels & Price, 2009).

The second comes from the oral tradition of panels created by the psychiatrist Claudio Naranjo at Berkeley in 1970. It consists of participating in a meeting with a panel of people that have the same dominate emotion and who share together in front of the group. The facilitator, through everyone's answers, brings to light the characteristics associated with the type, brought forward by the panel. It is striking to realize the close proximity of the thoughts, feelings and behaviors, as well as the similarity of the logic of the points of view expressed by the panelists embodying the same type. The degree of intensity with which you align yourself with the panel allows you to determine if you recognize yourself in this enneatype or not. This approach is very reliable, but requires a bit of time (ideally a weekend to attend nine panels).

The third is to do a "typing session" accompanied by a specialized coach. This kind of session lasts about two hours. The results depend on the capacity of the coach to let you find your own enneatype using a questionnaire that is subtle, comprehensive and controlled, and to not impose on you their own assessment of your type.

In any case, the key point to remember here is that each one of us is alone in being able to confirm our own enneatype.

In these various writings, my trainer and friend Marie-Claire Fagioli, management coach and pioneer of the Enneagram in Switzerland, summarizes, in a very concise way, the principal characteristics of each enneatype as follows (Fagioli, 2007):

"Type 1s, Perfectionists, are attentive to errors, to norms, to doing things right. Conscientious, you can count on them. However, their perfectionism can make them painstaking, critical or too demanding toward others or themselves. They can demonstrate a relative slowness, especially when it involves moving toward the unknown.

Type 2s, Altruists, like above all to be useful, even indispensable. They are helpful and warm. They take care of others, forgetting their own needs, and running the risk of seeming intrusive. If they don't receive enough recognition, they could not take it well and react aggressively.

Type 3s, Achievers, need to act and get results. They are sure of themselves, positive, good leaders and even a bit "carefree". Concerned about giving a good image of themselves, they do everything to avoid failure, or they conceal it. To succeed in their professional life the 3s risk doing too much and are at the mercy of health "issues".

Type 4s, Romantics, feel unique and different and they avoid banality. They are often brilliant and creative. At ease in emotional situations, they are looking for recognition. If they don't get enough, they appear arrogant at times and sure of themselves, sometimes subject to depression, which can make them unpredictable (or contradictory).

Type 5s, Observers, are often withdrawn and they like solitude. They are composed, almost unemotional, thanks to their capacity to keep their great fragility to themselves. Reflecting, understanding is their preferred activity. They don't speak a lot, but speak well, when their opinion is sought or when it concerns a subject in which they are considered specialized.

Type 6s, Loyal Skeptics, doubt, question, challenge. They are loyal, sensitive and helpful, ready to devote themselves to a cause that they esteem valid or to a solid and legitimate authority, and at times are dependent, at times rebellious. In a team, a 6 can play a (positive) role of safeguard, but they risk being taken as a pessimist.

Type 7s, Epicures, favor pleasure and freedom. They are fast and capable of succeeding at several tasks at a time. Curious to try everything, they are joyous, optimistic, active and enthusiastic. However, they can't bear routine and it is difficult to keep them from leaving if their job doesn't please them.

Type 8s, Leaders, are energetic, independent, uncompromising. They are impressive from (apparent) strength and assurance in themselves, because they avoid looking weak or vulnerable. They know how to take things in hand and are protective. They don't tolerate contradiction well. Others often think that they take up too much space.

Type 9s, Mediators, look for agreement and harmony. They are active, kind and hard workers. Concerned with everyone's wellbeing and good listeners, they contribute greatly to creating a good atmosphere. However, a conflict climate can quickly disturb them and make them worried, nervous and indecisive."

The model regroups these nine enneatypes in three triads presenting specific characteristics.

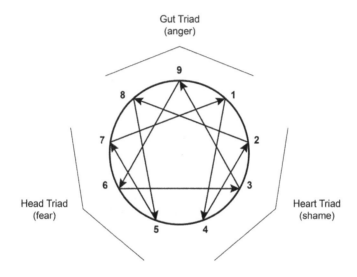

On one hand, each triad involves one of our three centers of intelligence: The Heart Triad deals with emotional intelligence for types 2, 3, 4; the Head Triad deals with mental intelligence for types 5, 6, 7; The Gut Triad deals with instinctive intelligence for types 8, 9, 1. It is interesting to note that in general, the dynamic of the Enneagram centers our personalities around *savoir*, *faire* and *être*.

This means, for example, that to make a decision, a 5, Observer, will start from an analytical reflection, while an 8, Leader, will mainly call upon instinct and a 4, Romantic, will follow their emotions. Of course, no one makes a decision 100% according to one of these diagrams, but each type will principally call upon their mental intelligence, instinct or intelligence of the heart.

On the other hand, our functioning is often dictated by our reaction to three emotions: shame, fear or anger.

Thus the triad (2, 3, 4) is particularly reactive to shame. However, each of these three types reacts differently. Type 2 overcomes it by wanting to be helpful, 3 looks for recognition, and 4 conquers it by wanting to be different. Likewise, triad (5, 6, 7) faces fear. Type 5 will avoid fear by isolating themselves. Type 6 will live with it by taming it. The Type 7 will free themselves from it and disperse. Finally, the triad (8, 9, 1) is sensitive to anger. Type 8 will express this by asserting themselves with force, Type 9 will deny it by putting the needs of others before their own and Type 1 will contain it and keep it under the surface.

Here also, these behaviors are not exclusive. For example, a 5 can of course become angry and a 9 can certainly feel fear. But each triad has its own way of functioning. One should also note that certain types, such as the 3 (Achiever), the 7 (Epicure) or the 8 (Leader) are notoriously optimistic.

How is this tool particularly useful in sales?

First of all, it allows you to better understand the way you function, your underlying motivations, how you make your choices and what type of interaction you establish with others.

Then, by recognizing the differences that exist between the types, you measure the diversity and richness of those that surround you. By giving you the keys to better understand others, the Enneagram opens the doors of empathy for you. It allows you to take a step back from yourself and to accept the others as they are.

Finally, the knowledge of the enneatype of others with whom you collaborate (family, colleagues, clients) gives you guidance for better communication and fruitful teamwork. It's true that it is difficult to precisely assess a person's enneatype who has not been "typed". So, a good knowledge of Enneagram basics and of your own enneatype, along with good listening and attentive observation of the person's behavior, will allow you to identify certain enneatype qualities of your intermediary.

As a result, you can make your exchanges more smooth and personalized. For example, by addressing an Observer (5), you just have to respect their precise and parsimonious answers; in working with a Mediator (9), don't push them around; when a project manager that is a Loyal Skeptic (6) makes you aware of everything that could not work in your project, listen without treating them as a defeatist: their "Jiminy Cricket" side will make you more careful and will help you avoid setbacks; finally, a tonic and ambitious proposition will be appreciated by an Achiever (3).

Ambition versus Ego

For me, Ambition is the motor that puts the bar high, even very high. It helps you build your dreams and shape your conviction that you can reach them. Ambition relies on the conviction that you are capable. It is what makes you say: "I can do it". It is a positive energy to get you started, to strive to do better, by working with others. In sales, you need to advance with your team to win the business, and along with your client to build together the best solution to meet their needs.

Ego, a noun from the Latin personal pronoun me/I, generally designates the awareness that one has of oneself. It is sometimes considered the foundation of personality (notably in psychology) or as an obstacle to our personal development (notably in spirituality). In this book, I use the word ego from the second viewpoint, meaning what one commonly calls a "big Ego", and will distinguish it with a capital E.

Today, this Ego is everywhere and it wreaks havoc. Ego is pretention, even the belief that you are better than the other person, that you "are worth" intrinsically more than him. And often, that other person is wrong, or bad. Ego does not position you as compared to yourself, but as compared to others. As such, it can be a powerful obstacle to self-development and reaching your full potential.

Political, religious, and military systems and management of numerous organizations unfortunately rely on the Ego. It is the breeding ground for what psychologists call narcissists, perverts or psychotics. It is one of the reasons that these systems lead to war, be it physical or economical.

In sales, the Ego is known to be a flaw when the salesperson esteems: "to know better than the client what is good for the client", when the salesperson talks too much and doesn't listen enough, believing to know and to have understood in the place of the client. This flaw is called arrogance. It leads to failure.

Hence my conclusion: The booster of excellence is Ambition. The destructor of excellence is Ego.

Ambition and Humility

One of the best ways to develop yourself and reach your objectives is to associate strong Ambition with great Humility. Humility reminds us that we are not perfect and thus we are perfectible. It helps you to learn, to question your plans, your beliefs, to take a step back with respect to your certitudes, to listen and to identify with others. Humility is a powerful motor for Empathy.

To grow, it is also important to be kind to yourself and to others. Accepting to go into ourselves to explore, with kindness, our values, our underlying motivations, our hidden personalities – which Carl Jung calls our shadow. The kinder you are with yourself, the longer you can go deep inside yourself. It is the same with your clients: the kinder you are with them, the better you will get to know them. Also, the stronger your Ambition is, the more your progression will increase. Whether it be your personal or professional advancement.

Historically, professional advancement follows an S curve. We begin in a discipline as a "junior" then as we continue to practice it we become an "advanced professional" and finally when we fully master it we become a "senior". It is at this moment that the curve might invert, and if we don't do anything, we stagnate, even descend along with it.

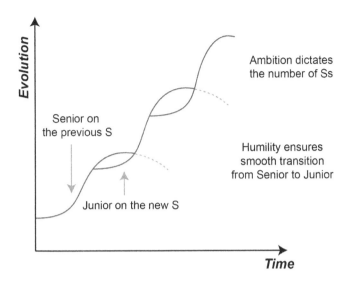

Ambition & Humility

Between the end of World War 2 and the middle of the 80s, an entire career could spread out over a single S curve. Each phase lasted between five to fifteen years. Today, an S curve lasts about five years and each phase (junior, advanced, senior) lasts between one to two years.

This acceleration obliges us to progress by having several mini "careers" in S. It is in the moving between each S that humility plays a crucial role, because we must accept leaving a "senior" position to become "junior" on the next curve. From "master" we become "beginner". Our status and our position changes. We are called into question. We must abandon (in part) what we know to gain new knowledge, unlearn to move forward to new instruction, leave our position to adopt new behaviors.

In two words, you have to "let go"; but let go in order to get further ahead.

The number of S depends on our Ambition. The bigger it is, the more we will look for new opportunities to grow, to develop, to do new things, to take new responsibilities, to face new challenges, then the more S there will be.

The speed of passing from one S to another depends on our Humility. The better you tame your Ego and develop your Humility, knowing toward which goal your Ambition is leading you, the more your rise toward this goal will be smooth.

Moreover, certain companies don't leave us the choice. When we are recognized as having high potential, the company forces us to move along this pattern. It is what one of my mentors called "to be subject to strategic discomfort".

Speaking of mentors, Humility allows you to recognize those who are really excellent, to admire their skills and know-how, and to appreciate their *savoir-être* and to take lessons from it. Observe them. Approach them. Copy them. Not to mimic them or to lose your identity, but to learn from the best source. You will be surprised to realize how accessible the best ones are. And ready to help you. They know that life is short. They know that you also would like to achieve your ambitions. And it's only by approaching them that you give yourself the means to do so.

Key take-aways

- Identify your SWOT and work on it

- Find a mentor and, if possible, a coach

- Understand the Enneagram and find your enneatype

- Be ambitious and let go of your Ego, to get further ahead

- Be humble and kind to yourself, to grow

- Dare to make several "S" in your career and in your life

CHAPTER 4

SELLING STARTS WHEN THE CUSTOMER SAYS NO!

I often say that the sale starts when the client says "no". It's not by provocation and it's not to make the act of selling more difficult than it is. What I mean to say is that if a client tells you yes right away, or very quickly, you are not in the process of selling. It is the client that is buying.

When you enter into a butcher's shop, you are going to buy meat, not fish. The butcher doesn't need to convince you of the advantages of meat over fish. As long as their product satisfies you, you will buy it there, even if the butcher is grouchy or not very nice and even if their shop is a bit far away. Maybe the first time you went there, the butcher "sold" you their meat, but since then, it's you who has been buying.

In a different setting, a long time ago, the client of one of my colleagues, Nicole, bought a certain kind of computer from one of our best competitors. The client liked the product and it was of good quality. In addition, as the client purchased a big quantity, the price was very competitive. At first, our competitor had most certainly made big efforts to win the business. Then the process of transactional sales was put in place: each month the client received an email with the available configurations. The client just had to check the desired configuration, indicate the required quantity then send back the order. The "sale" was done. In fact, a "transaction" took place each month. Our competitor was no longer selling anything. It was the client that was buying. Nicole and her team did their best to demonstrate, over at least a year, that our technical features were better, but nothing worked. She systematically received a polite "no", until the day that she introduced the notion of service into the equation. Because of this client's very high level of technical competencies, all of the services for configuration, installation, interlinking and implementation were completely handled by the client's teams. We had just recruited several engineers specialized in this area. Thanks to her contacts, Nicole proposed to the client's IT management to study together the break-even point at which it would be more advantageous to outsource these services. The client went along and our teams worked together on a Total Cost of Ownership. While the competitor's price was unknown to us, the client's growing involvement convinced Nicole that she could put together an integrated solution comprising all of the services, the material and software, for a lower global cost than the budget used.

In addition, this freed the client's teams for other tasks more in line with their core business. A call for tender was issued. Our competitor was taken by surprise. Not benefiting from a strong relationship with the client or from recruitment in services, the competitor made an irrelevant proposal. Nicole and her team won the business by progressively replacing more than 150 servers as part of a three-year service contract, with a possible two-year extension. The sale made by Nicole began when her client told her "no".

This is why sales is, above all, a mindset. One of not accepting – in theory – things as they are. One of not stopping at the first contradiction, the first aggravation. One of looking at the bigger picture when faced with a refusal. One of understanding what is beyond appearances, understanding others, their motivations and their reasons for accepting or refusing what is proposed to them. Understand the *Why (i.e. the reasons)* behind their refusal and the *What (i.e. the purposes)* of their need, their project or their strategy. One of putting yourself in their place by putting on their glasses, entering into their perception, vision and way of functioning. This mindset is based on Empathy, a quality and competence that is essential in sales that we have already addressed in the preceding chapter. Let us remember that Empathy is the capacity to mentally identify with others and to understand their feeling or point of view. I insist on the term competence, because Empathy can be learned and developed. Like all other competencies, even if it is beneficial to have certain predispositions at the beginning, it can be learned on the condition that you have the desire, humility, patience and discipline.

Nevertheless, developing your Empathy takes time. It is part of *savoir-être*, because it relies on your deep values, the way you will consider others, your capacity to "put yourself in their shoes" to understand their feelings, what they think and what they are planning.

The non-violent communication workshops that we will address in Chapter 7 offer an excellent place to practice opening up to others and to enter into empathy with people you don't know. This is particularly useful during the initial contact phase with new clients.

In fact, Empathy is at the heart of all sales success. If I were to summarize in a few words: Empathy is to Negotiation what Charisma is to Leadership.

Negotiation begins when you say "Hello!"

Here we come to the question about the place of negotiation in the sales process. Contrary to widespread thought, sales is an element of the negotiation process, and not the reverse. Negotiation begins when you say "Hello!" to your client. The way you present yourself, the way you establish the first contact and engage in the first discussions, will position you very quickly in your client's mind and in their perception of the relationship that could develop between you. Even if this perception in not initially conscious, it develops very quickly and will determine, to a large extent, the emotions that will subsequently be expressed during the course of the sales relationship.

Of course, this process occurs in the same way for you. The initial perception you have of your client and the emotional, intellectual and instinctive positioning that you will establish in your relationship with him happens very quickly.

Yet, the question of buying or selling something hasn't even come up! The selling will begin later, when a need has been expressed, a solution starts to be put together and a common desire to cooperate is confirmed, without a commitment to signing a contract and finalizing a deal. However, negotiations have already started.

It is during the first contact that you and your client will subconsciously begin to position yourselves. It is difficult to say how much time this positioning will take. It depends on each person's experience and capacity to put things into perspective. Considerable experience allows one to quickly see who you are dealing with. A high capacity to take a global view avoids giving in to hasty judgment to allow time to see how the relationship develops. In any case, this positioning happens relatively quickly at the beginning of the relationship and once in place, it is difficult to change it.

Managing this first contact effectively is therefore essential, in particular with clients that are important and not easily available, such as the members of general management.

Three vital facts prevail over the negotiation process and its success: the perception of your client, the trust that you inspire and your capacity to maintain this trust.

Their perception is their reality

We have just looked at the importance and the role that perception plays at the beginning of establishing a sales relationship. Americans tend to say: "perception is reality". However, this wording is incorrect because it is extreme. On the other hand, it is true that "perception is the reality of the perceiver". Perception is relative to the observer. Two observers – each being rational or well intentioned – can have very different perceptions of the same event. The difference in statements by accident witnesses is a very good example.

This fact can lead to untimely false judgments, regrettable mistakes, missed opportunities, costly errors, and irreparable ruptures or deadly conflicts. It is obvious that

Ego, with all of its shortcomings, intensifies these slip-ups.

However, we can also use perception in a constructive way. By being open, kind and sincere, we lead our client to be so as well. We guide their perception in a positive way, toward us, toward building a relationship and establishing trust. We bring about a beneficial mirror effect for the two parties.

Observation of gestures, what we call body language, is one of the many tools for putting in place this mirror effect. The effect consists of adopting mannerisms similar to those of your client. This creates a behavioral resonance that puts the two parties at ease. It requires a bit of time to master this skill and to become natural at it to avoid giving the impression that you are imitating your partner. Conversely, your gestures can influence the other person, in particular, when you are calm and serene during difficult negotiations. Yawning is a well-known example of the mirror effect.

Certain people see this as manipulation. In fact, it's about creating favorable conditions for setting up a context for smooth dialogue. It is like the controlled adjustment of their tones of voice by two intermediaries during a discussion. Without control, the discussion could become cacophonous. Thanks to this, it remains under control.

Kindness versus Trust

Americans always say: "People buy from people they like". Even if there is some truth in the saying that one buys more easily from someone who is nice it is more appropriate to say: "People buy from people they trust". You can be a very nice person, but if you don't inspire trust, it's unlikely that you will close deals.

This is one of the reasons that sales is sometimes poorly perceived. Too many people have placed their trust in someone and were disappointed. Whether they were taken advantage of or if they let themselves be taken advantage of doesn't change anything. It is therefore essential to develop a well-deserved position of trust, built upon the repetition of small events that reinforce this trust day after day.

The power of Trust

Trust is built over several months… and can be destroyed within a few seconds. This truth is obvious. And yet, it is too often disregarded. For example, as trust is established, certain beginner salespeople avoid saying things that could be disturbing to their clients, because they are afraid of damaging this trust and thus they adopt counterproductive behavior. Instead of using the freedom that the established trust has afforded them, they restrain and forbid themselves from using the strength of their sincerity. Yet trust is truly attained when one can (almost) say anything.

Trust is built on a foundation of three main components: sincerity, respect and empathy.

By being sincere, your client knows that they can count on you and that you firmly believe in what you are proposing. They may not always agree with you, but they know that you are telling the truth. This starts a dialogue that is honest, open and enriching. Sincerity enables you to build together on a sound basis.

Respect provides your client with a protected interpersonal space. It enables and encourages him to reveal himself. Confidentiality can be established.

Empathy creates a compassionate communication environment and reinforces the protected interpersonal space established by respect. If empathy is a great tool for understanding the feelings or the point of view of your contact, sound knowledge of the Enneagram, presented in the previous chapter, can make you attentive to their communication style and automatic behaviors and give you indications of their deeper motivations.

By being sincere, showing respect and expressing empathy, trust is developed on a solid foundation. This process is a virtuous circle that is built over time as we reinforce each of its elements.

Trust at the heart of the customer experience

In order to illustrate the power of trust and the key role it plays in the customer experience, let me share with you what I experienced with my car dealership. A few years ago I was won over by a magnificent coupé that had just been announced at the Paris Automobile Show. The manufacturer assured me that the model would be available in Switzerland in three months. As my car had just broken down I decided to rent a car during these three months. In reality, the rental lasted one year. I decided, obviously, to look at cars from the competition, but this unrelentingly brought me back to my preferred model because of the commitment of Eric, the salesperson from my car dealership. He called me every month to keep me informed on the progress of technical trials (i.e. the coupé introduced a new four-wheel drive technology) and marketing plans (i.e. the brand was targeting a new customer segment), and to inquire about my comparisons with the competition. At a crucial point, the director of the agency got involved to confirm that they would maintain the original price, which had increased, and that they would reimburse the two last months of my temporary car rental. Finally I acquired the much-awaited model, at the initial price and according to the desired configuration. Thanks to Eric's perseverance and to the trust created through a sincere and respectful relationship, I remained loyal to my dealership and to his brand.

However, the business didn't stop there. When I created a company in the thermal heating sector we needed five vans. Without comparing with other brands I went back to my dealership and bought five vehicles. It's not the vehicle technology or design that made the difference, it was my emotional commitment to this dealership that was created by an exceptional salesperson.

How to co-build a partnership?

If trust is a magnificent structure built patiently from the three bricks of sincerity, respect and empathy, it is essential that our Ego does not add in the least bit of dynamite. Because one way to break down trust is to practice sales like it's an arm wrestling match. The pressure to reach quarterly result objectives and expectations from management, who themselves are subject to those of the hierarchy, who are subject to the shareholders, makes us lose the sense of reality. This pressure, when combined with a lack of business maturity, pushes certain salespeople to display hostility, disregard the rules of business conduct, draft poorly constructed contracts or make promises that can't be kept. In short, they transform their business space into a boxing ring.

Sometimes managers require their sales teams to go up the hierarchy of an important client in order to sign a big contract just before the end of the quarter. Doing all that is possible to sign a contract in time is normal practice in sales. To go around one's main contact to scale their hierarchy is no longer sales, but sales harassment. It is absurd and an absolute lack of business know-how. It makes obvious the loss of a sense of reality by certain sales executives who forget that it is the client that keeps them alive and that you don't bite the hand that feeds you.

The market pressure is there. It's an undeniable fact. It has a tendency to increase with the effect of globalization, market fragmentation, the increase in the number of competitors, and from the immediacy and the delocalization made available by technology.

Our clients are subject to the same pressures. They also have priorities, deadlines and constraints dictated by their own clients, managers and shareholders. Each party must protect their interests.

It is here that the notion of a genuine partnership takes on its meaning. Before going further, I must specify what I mean by partnership because this word is quite overused. *Being a partner is helping the other to do their business over the long-term.* In this regard, a partnership is built jointly by pooling the energy and the resources of the two parties to develop together the best solution for the needs of your client and to reach your sales objectives.

One of the major principles for efficient co-building is to integrate your teams with your client's and to channel the energy of the resulting team on the most important things.

The same as for a couple, developing joint projects to establish partnership requires thinking long-term and acting short-term. Here is where I would like to introduce an approach that will allow you to co-build a structured sales plan with your client over the long-term. This approach presents a business strategy based on the simultaneous management of three time horizons to create growth, inspired by the book *The Alchemy of Growth* (Baghai *et al*, 2000).

Think long-term, act short-term

It's about building a strategy that is based on three time horizons covering different periods but beginning at the same time. Horizon 1 covers the first time unit; Horizon 2 covers two time units; and Horizon 3 covers three time units.

In general, the time unit is a year. But in certain sectors, the unit can be shorter, for example, six months, or longer, such as eighteen months. In summary, it's about planting to harvest at precise moments in the short, medium and long-term. The longer the horizon is, the more it will address sales projects on a greater strategic scale. This will involve contacts at higher and higher levels in department management, general management or even the board of directors.

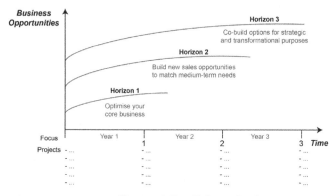

The strategic Three Horizons sales plan

Here is how to develop your sales strategy:

To build Horizon 1, which targets the short-term, you will concentrate on defending your core business, which is based on the products or services that your company already sells to this client. Horizon 1 aims to generate cash immediately with the products currently being sold and/or services in process of being implemented, all while allowing new doors to be opened with your client.

You will build your Horizon 2, which begins today but targets the medium-term encompassing the extension of your core business, by proposing more complex solutions. For example, if you currently sell devices, you can develop service offers centered on these devices or look for partners to enrich your current offer, or find new internet channels to sell more or explore the needs of units other than that of your current contact. The idea is to find solutions outside of your usual sales context in order to increase the reach of your territory, the amount of your sales revenue and to get ahead of the competition. Horizon 2 opens a new area of diversification by targeting sales around solutions and not only products and/or standard services.

Horizon 3 aims at strategic long-term projects. To build this horizon you have to *Think Big*! You have to *Be Very Ambitious*! For your customer, for your company and for you. Whether it be an exclusive five-year contract, your client's business model transformation project, or the creation of a new project involving research and development, these projects stimulate innovation, a seamless alliance and a strong willingness to collaborate together. It requires time, investment and commitment as much on the part of your client's general management as your own. Horizon 3 opens an area of innovation and enables you to work on what is at the heart of your client's identity. At the same time, it allows time and offers the opportunity for your company to explore new concepts, gain new skills and to develop new technologies, new products and services. It seals a true partnership with your client.

Such a sales strategy presents numerous advantages, in particular if you are in charge of the overall relationship with clients with complex needs or large governmental or multinational organizations.

1. It targets long-term right from the beginning. You begin to work on these three horizons at the same time, and work on each in parallel, but at different paces.

2. It allows you to increase the number of contacts with your client. This gives access to in-depth knowledge of the organization, its various needs and operations. This substantially boosts your opportunities for new business.

3. It allows you to participate in your client's strategic transformation by opening the door to innovation, whether it be technological, organizational or related to your client's business model. It also stimulates your company to explore new ideas, create new wealth and prepare its own future.

4. It brings you a structured context and a road map that you can share with your team and with your client. It acts as a compass for objectives that you will regularly refine with your client. In sharing it with them, you will integrate their short-, medium- and long-term vision. It will delineate the steps that you and your client's teams will reach together. This will naturally solidify a strong collaboration.

5. It is a dynamic process. In this sense, it is a perfect illustration of one of the fundamental pillars of negotiation – Process – which we will look at in the next chapter: if you are in agreement with your client on a Three Horizon plan, you will find agreement on the architecture of your relationship with him. You can develop and deepen relationships with your usual contacts and expand to new ones. Finally you can co-build a solution based on time frames adapted to their needs.

6. It aims to generate profitable growth. The growth must come from a number of new opportunities, which the strategy allows you to discover or generate. If your company sells several product or service ranges, a

Three Horizon deployment opens multiple opportunities. It enables you to avoid putting everything in the same basket and not depend on only one source of revenue. By creating a mix between your products and/or services you can manage these sales opportunities like a diversified portfolio between stock, bonds and cash.

Nevertheless, a structured sales strategy over the long-term and based on a solid alliance is a necessary condition, but not sufficient, to ensure profitable growth for you. You also need quality products and/or services with indisputable added value. My strategy professor at IMD, Professor Fred Neubaeur used to say: "If you don't earn money, it's because you have a bad strategy or you are in the wrong business".

Last but not least, this strategy allows you to envision your business with serenity. Which does not mean in a slow or sluggish way. There will be discouraging phases and euphoric phases. Phases during which you will earn a lot of money and others when you will earn less. That is life! But this strategy will allow you to stay on a course that is solid and shared with your client.

Co-build with sharing and participating

Here are some other examples of client engagement in the interest of the two parties. If you have a presentation to do for your client's management or team, have him read through your first draft, test your arguments with him, ask for their feedback and adapt your presentation accordingly.

If you have a presentation to do for your management or your team, invite your client to do the presentation introduction, to present their strategy and priorities, to point out the areas of potential partnership and share what they expect from your company, from you and your team.

On one hand, your client feels valued by the active listening and interest from the main representatives of your company. On the other hand, your management and your team are motivated by the direct access to one of the strategic decision makers of your client. Finally, it helps you gain precious time by drawing directly from the source the key elements that you and your team will work on.

Also involve your client's team in everything that your team does for him. If a new solution is developed, put together – if possible – a joint team to co-build the solution. I say "if possible" because there are sectors, such as public administration, that forbid contacts with potential suppliers during the tendering stage. In this case, you need to establish good collaboration before the tendering has begun in order to anticipate future needs and prepare together for the opportunities to come. Furthermore, regardless of the sector in consideration, the client always maintains the freedom of involvement that they wish to accord.

The advantages of co-building the solution are numerous. Establishing a solution must, in general, respond to a requirements specification; it requires time, data, and filling in the blanks. A joint team allows you to have access to high quality information, to clarify unclear areas, to find and/or refine ideas, to keep a good pace, a dynamic and an enthusiasm, to know one another, to better understand each other, to appreciate one another, to communicate smoothly, quickly and precisely, to correct one another, to improve and to share points of view, habits and different cultures.

By getting involved in the development of the solution, the client commits and becomes co-responsible for the quality of the solution. This will influence their final choice.

In addition, the devil is in the detail… missing elements, or on the contrary those that are unnecessary, in the initial request can be updated during this joint work. By working together, you will notice, over time, if the development is going in the right direction, thanks to the feedback from your client. If this is not the case, it will be easier and faster to make things right.

The necessity of a sponsor

No matter the size of your client's company, it has its own culture with rituals, practices, habits and things left unsaid. Its organization chart shows the public face of the organization, but does not at all reflect who has the real power, who influences in the shadows, who makes the decisions and who takes the decision. There is the implementation of a strategy and the development of one underway, current priorities and those to come, changes underway and those in preparation. It is essential to understand these factors, some of which are decisive for your business and its long-term relationship with your client.

In fact, you need a sponsor within your client's company. Someone to guide you in this maze, someone who is placed high enough to have an overall view of the present and the future, with enough power to take, to have taken or to influence the decisions concerning your business, and – above all – someone who you completely trust and who completely trusts you.

When a relationship has been well established with respect, empathy and sincerity, it is ready to be transformed into sponsorship.

On a more global scale, make your sponsor visible within your company and take advantage of their position and power within their company. At times, crucial decisions are taken in a few seconds based on an encounter, an exchange or synergy between two people.

By making your sponsor visible within your company, you increase the opportunities for such encounters and exchanges at a high level. In return, by soliciting their help, you can get access to levels of management that would otherwise be difficult to reach.

I often used these two approaches simultaneously by putting my internal and external sponsors in contact. In particular, when we were *not* in an intense commercial phase. This allowed us to create a more relaxed relationship, without ulterior motives, and without business pressure. These encounters, which required quite a bit of preparation, often brought around the table the client's CEO. The discussions were essentially private, sprinkled from time to time with business or strategic elements.

Decision maker vs. decision taker

Identifying who "makes" the decision and who "takes" the decision is essential for successfully navigating your client's maze of power. It was in disregarding this fundamental rule that I took my biggest "fall" in sales. At the beginning of my career, I had succeeded in establishing an excellent relationship with the IT director of the Swiss subsidiary of an international group. Over a six month period our teams had worked together to design the architecture of a decentralized IT network that covered the needs of one hundred agencies around the country. This network interconnected a hundred computers with a revolutionary hardware architecture at the time and a size perfectly adapted to the agencies. The IT director, a man with extensive experience and very well appreciated by his general management, had chosen the best, in terms of technology and in terms of optimizing investment costs. On my side, my proposition had been approved by my national and European management, and was cited as an example for its elegance. Everything was finally ready and our two national management groups were meeting for the signature of the contract that represented tens of millions of dollars.

When we arrived, the IT director told me that he had a slight problem. The previous day, the group's IT director had asked him for a few additional details about our very innovative technology but said it would just delay the signature by one week… In fact, the contract was never signed… My contact decided to leave his company… my annual results were catastrophic… and I understood, but too late, that I had worked in perfect unison with the person that made the decision and that I had completely ignored the one that really took the decision. In hindsight, it is obvious that I should have personally assured myself that the group's management had given their approval. In any case, it was a memorable lesson that taught me a lot!

It is, however, not always easy to determine who really decides in the end as opposed to those that make the decisions. Your sponsor can help you a lot in this regard.

The three pillars of successful negotiation

An experience at INSEAD provided me with the essence of negotiation. The teaching from Professor Horacio Falcao was invaluable to me to be able to succeed in important negotiations in both my personal and professional life. He advocates that the core of all formal negotiations is based on three fundamental pillars: *Relationship, Content and Communication* (Falcao, 2010).

The Three Pillars of Negotiation

Relationships create Trust. They are built on the different elements that we already outlined for establishing a climate of trust. Content generates Value. It concerns the subject of the agreement to be formulated during the negotiation. Communication dictates the Process. This process might define, for example, who the participants will be, the location and the frequency of meetings and the protocols and rules to be followed.

When one asks an audience of managers and salespeople which of these three pillars the priority should be given to, most of them will answer Relationship. In fact, the pillar that priority should be given to is Process, for these three reasons:

1. By agreeing to the process, we at least agree on something, right from the beginning.

2. A process is rational and not emotional. It sets a framework and a structure, which does not commit either of the parties to the result to be reached. In general, the two parties don't have any problems doing this. The task can and must be done as of the first meeting. If the two parties cannot agree on the process it means that there is a serious problem from the start.

3. A process allows you to calmly establish, from the beginning, the rules to follow when the negotiation becomes more difficult, the climate deteriorates, emotions emerge and Egos swell. Thus, it is important to quickly establish the arbitration procedures by higher decision-making bodies, the break procedures allowing each party to withdraw to reflect on their own without it

blocking the negotiation, and the negotiation exit procedure. The process also allows for the establishment of specific procedures to protect against the arrival of new participants when negotiations are underway, and/or unilateral introduction of new rules, which could fully challenge them.

Following a death in the family, one of my best friends was to manage the inheritance situation, which seemed to be quickly moving toward conflict. I gave him two pieces of advice: the first was to ask each party involved to take on a lawyer, in order to avoid the standoff of Egos and their emotions, and thus preserve, as much as possible, good family relations. The second was to ask the lawyers to use an Excel table to confirm, at each meeting, the value of assets, all while keeping a trace of the preceding versions. This routine procedure apparently made the lawyers laugh at first. In the end, it was only the table that was the key element of the arbitrage handled by the notary. And the family conflict was avoided.

This personal advice came from the simple rule that my teams and myself have always insisted on, to keep a record of decisions and share it with our client's interlocutors after each meeting. This often allowed us to refocus the debates and not let ourselves get caught up in the frequent diverging interpretations of each one.

In addition to the importance of processes, my friend's example also illustrates that a good relationship established with your usual interlocutors is not necessarily sufficient: new players can arrive, with whom you haven't had prior contact, inviting themselves to the negotiation table (lawyers, professional negotiators, external consultants, managers from other divisions, etc.). A new relationship must be established with them. It will probably be more official than one established outside of the formal context of the negotiations and it will take some time.

A rule to be respected scrupulously throughout the negotiations is to not mix these three pillars. You must be clear with each one of them and not try to have them interfere. For example, do not use the relationship that one could have with one or more of the interlocutors of the other party to infringe the rules of the process underway. Or do not use the process to force the way content is being created for the benefit of one of the parties.

Facts, just the facts, only the facts

The last fundamental point of good communication is to absolutely stop believing, thinking, imagining, assuming, guessing, etc. You must base everything on the facts, just the facts and only the facts! To do this, you must interrogate, verify, go from open questions (why, for what purpose, how) to closed questions (yes/no). The reformulation is a valuable aide to assure yourself and show your interlocutor that you have understood. If this is not the case, it will lead them to specify their point of view and thoughts. In this respect, confirm and have things confirmed in writing at the end of a meeting to avoid all misinterpretations.

Not believing, thinking, imagining, assuming, guessing, or interpreting, requires letting go of your beliefs and approaching the situation in an open and humble manner. Relying on facts, just the facts and only the facts anchors you on solid ground. For example, when your client vehemently asserts: "your product is much too expensive" or "you are 20% more expensive than your competitors", it is questions such as "what is your supporting basis to say that?" or "how did you arrive at that conclusion?" that will allow you to avoid the trap and provide you with specific elements that you can work with.

What should you focus on to win a sale?

To put all the odds on your side and win the sale, you must adopt a strategic mindset, take the right attitude and use your negotiating skills. Let's examine each of these points, one by one.

Adopt a strategic mindset

Strategic means long-term. For this you must have your own vision. Use the Three Horizons approach that we looked at previously. Identify ambitious themes and strategies for each horizon that you believe in, which make sense for your client and show your support for them.

Include a subject or a project dedicated to innovation in your vision. Using innovation is the best way to access the essence of your client and their upper management. It stimulates your creativity and that of your company, forces you to enhance and adapt your products and services and form a powerful differentiator from the competition. At times, the innovation that your company can bring is so unique that your competitors disappear from the screen.

Prepare yourself for any high-powered negotiations with your mentor and/or the director of your company who is the sponsor of your client (i.e. Primary Executive Partner), if your company has nominated one. They will challenge you on strategic aspects that you have not necessarily thought about, will bring you to reflect deeply and adopt a posture that is aligned with the senior management of your client.

Think long-term, act short-term. This is the definition of a truly strategic mindset. Thinking long-term strengthens your approach over time. It will give you the perspective, strength and serenity to do quality work. Acting short-term builds your approach in a moment. Thus, you measure the progressive development of what is accomplished, day by day, nourishing your motivation and commitment.

Never lose sight of the famous three inescapable facts, which are:

- Your client's perception is their reality.

- If people buy from people they like, executives buy from people they trust.

- Trust is built over several months… and can be destroyed in only a few minutes.

Adopt the right attitude

Identify your partner's profile. Are they more task- and activity-oriented, or rather people- and team-oriented? Do they easily adopt a global view, or prefer focusing on the details? Are they more conceptual than pragmatic? Are they visual or auditory?

Be proactive, confident, and provocative. It's not about being unnecessarily provocative or bothering your contact. It's about making him react in a constructive way. To do this, you have two well-known magic questions: "Why?" and "How?" Why do you do this…? Why don't you do that…? How do you do this…? How would you do that…?

A third magic question is "For which purpose?" What is the objective…? What are your intentions in doing this…? Or in not doing that…?

Be humble. Be sincere. And use your empathy. At the risk of repeating myself, these attitudes are essential for increasing your excellence in sales. They are unfortunately underestimated, ignored or mishandled.

Say what you do, do what you say. It is interesting to note that the practice of this rule, which is easier to say than to do, leads you to be sincere. Because it obligates you, on one hand, to commit yourself, and on the other, to respect your commitments, and so you learn how to formulate them by thinking about them two times (at least!). Conversely, the more sincere you are, the easier this rule, which is widely appreciated, is to put into practice.

Use your negotiating skills

When the time to really negotiate draws near, apply the three pillars of negotiation that we have just detailed by always beginning with agreement on the process. This constitutes the foundation of your entire negotiation architecture on which you will progressively build the relationship and the content. Remember that the negotiation process started the day you said "Hello" to your client, and the sales phase itself is only an element of the negotiation process. Everything that has happened since the beginning of your first encounter with your client influences the moment when you are going to truly enter into discussion for a specific sale.

This observation shows how important it is to recollect past events that you can use to make connections and comparisons between comments, observations, questions, and even confidential information that your client has shared. Search your memory for all the elements that could help explain the meaning of the words and actions of your interlocutors.

Just as we have already discussed, keep in mind to stick to the facts, just the facts and only the facts. Facts keep emotions at a distance and refocus the discussion. On your side, be specific and concise. If you don't know, say so; don't let things become ambiguous, neither with your client or yourself.

Finally, there is a golden rule to respect: never sell through an intermediary. If your salary depends on the sale, you are responsible for closing it. You can delegate actions, call in all kinds of necessary skills that are useful and complementary to your own, but you must never, in any case, delegate the responsibility to be present at key moments of the sale, and in particular, at its conclusion.

During the whole sales process, there are a number of points on which you must agree, and the number of participants in the decision can prove to be high. As we have discussed previously, there is on one side the decision "makers", those that "know what is needed" or use the product, such as the end users that work with a new accounting software, the adolescent who has a very specific idea about the tablet that they want, or one of the spouses that wants this or that car model. On the other side, there are the decision "takers", who hold the purse strings or the overall authority required. Nevertheless, you must win multiple victories with several interlocutors. It's the accumulation of these various agreements that will progressively lead to putting the client in a good disposition to take a final decision, in favor of your proposition. It could be that one of these agreements is the one that tilts the balance completely in your favor. Because it can be difficult to predict when this will happen, it is important to prepare for this possibility. By putting into practice the advice given in this book, by sharpening your sensitivity, your instinct and your empathy, you will know when things are in the process of being decided. At that moment, it is crucial to let go, to let things happen and… to remain silent. This attitude is inspired by the technique that Lord Beaverbrook recommended to Winston Churchill in order to get appointed Prime Minister in 1940 in place of Lord Halifax.

This episode, reported by Françoise Giroud in her work *Si je mens* (*If I lie*) is very enlightening (Giroud, 1972). While Chamberlain designated Lord Halifax to succeed him, he asked Churchill to be number two in the government during a private interview. Churchill, out of patriotism, accepted. A few hours later, his friend Lord Beaverbrook, an English media mogul gifted with formidable business intelligence, having unofficially learned of the news, urged him to go back on his decision and to demand the position of Prime Minister because "only you can mobilize Great Britain". Churchill knows that Beaverbrook is right, but he gave his word and refuses to discuss it. Lord Beaverbrook tells him: "I ask you only one thing. When you are summoned by Chamberlain with Halifax and he asks you to confirm your acceptance, remain silent for three minutes. Three full minutes. One-hundred and eighty seconds. Before saying yes. In the name of England, I ask you!" Churchill finds the idea ridiculous and doesn't see how it could change the situation, but he has friendship and esteem for Beaverbrook. He promises to do as he asks.

The next day, Churchill and Halifax are in Chamberlain's office. And Chamberlain says: "Would you please confirm to Lord Halifax that you accept joining his cabinet?" And Churchill is silent. One minute. One and a half minutes. He remains silent. Before the three minutes are up, Lord Halifax says: "I think that it is Winston Churchill that should be Prime Minister". And Françoise Giroud concludes: "The least we can say is that these three minutes played a major role in the history of the Second World War".

Applying this attitude to sales consists of asking at the right moment: "Do you see an objection to closing on this point?" then be silent and wait. Wait one minute, two minutes, three minutes… the time it takes. But above all, do not break your silence. In fact, it is the one who breaks the silence that bends to the will of the other. If your client speaks first, it is very likely that they agree to move forward with your proposition. If you speak first, you risk calling everything into question. Staggeringly simple in appearance, it is extremely efficient… and very difficult to do. It requires self-observation, self-control and practice. However, silence is an undeniably formidable asset in numerous negotiations, whether it concerns weekend outings when confronted with mediocre school grades, the choice for the next vacation, your salary increase or your session tomorrow with your favorite client. Whatever the context, control your emotions and... be silent!

You now understand better why you must not delegate the responsibility to be present in key moments of the sales process and, in particular, its conclusion. It is also wise to brief your colleagues on this technique when they join you with a client. Why does it work? Why does one who remains silent have more of a chance of winning the game? Is it the discomfort in face of silence? Emotional instability that prevails over the rationale? I don't know. However, it works more often than expected, so try it. After all, keeping silent doesn't hurt anyone, and if it allows you to win big, it could really be worth it!

Key take-aways

- Negotiation begins when you say "Hello!"

- The sale begins when your client tells you "No!"

- Trust = Sincerity + Respect + Empathy

- Empathy is asking what would I do "if I were them"

- Begin by agreeing on the process

- Co-build a partnership with your client

- Use the 3 Horizons to co-build a business strategy over the long-term

- Find a sponsor from within your client's company

- Identify who "makes" the decision and who "takes" the decision

- Involve your client and their team in everything that you do for them

- Rely on the facts, just the facts and only the facts

- Be uniquely responsible for concluding your sales

- Use silence wisely

CHAPTER 5

SELLING IS COACHING YOUR CUSTOMER

The starting point of all successful sales relationships, by which I mean, regularly concluding sales over the long-term, is what I call Alliance, a concept borrowed from the worlds of psychology and coaching. Alliance is based on two major ingredients: mutual trust and joint projects. It crystallizes when mutual trust serves a joint project that is the result of a need expressed by your client and your capacity to bring together a solution. By creating a framework in which your client knows they can trust you, that their needs are understood and that their interests are respected, Alliance becomes the relationship base on which you and your client will co-build a long-term partnership.

As we saw in the previous chapter, trust in a sales relationship is based on sincerity, respect and empathy. Perhaps this is due to the fact that I am French, but I see a profound parallel between a sales relationship and an amorous relationship. Both go through three important phases: seduction, union and communal life. Like for a couple, communal life can continue over a long period of time but it can also end with a temporary or definitive separation, either because of a competitor or because of bad management of the relationship.

In any case, to be a good salesperson you must fundamentally "love" your client. Why? Because the essence of your relationship will mainly call upon emotions. Each party must want to go toward the other, to collaborate with the other, to succeed together, to build together, over the long-term. A short-term view is deadly for a true sales relationship. In business as well, a short-lived relationship can be pleasant at the moment but go nowhere. During a joint project, you will have to fight together, overcome frustrations, phases of discouragement and worry. You need to understand how each one operates, if possible anticipate each other's needs, reactions and demands. You will need to agree and to be patient. You will also have to celebrate together the joint victory represented by the signature of a contract, which is the fruit of hours, weeks, maybe even months of negotiations, or the end of a successful project.

As Antoine de Saint Exupéry said: "Love does not consist of gazing at each other, but in looking outward together in the same direction". In business, it is Alliance, this mix of mutual trust and joint projects, that is the essential ingredient to begin, maintain and make fruitful a healthy and successful sales relationship over the long-term.

Help me to help you

Today our clients are quite educated and very well informed. Purchasing directors know the range of sales techniques like the back of their hand and with a simple click of the mouse all managers can easily access your product features and those of your competition. In many cases your client knows your products better than you and most of the time they know your competitor's products better than you. This is why salespeople need to have good knowledge of the underlying technology of what they are selling, or to be accompanied by skilled specialists.

The globalization of exchanges, the rise of geopolitical ideologies and the continuous emergence of new technologies, increases the complexity of the world. The result is that the economic context becomes more and more unstable, changes are deeper and faster and the risks are greater. The facets of the present are diversifying and the parameters are multiplying and becoming entangled. The future is becoming more uncertain and difficult to predict. More and more managers believe that these changes are structural and so likely to endure.

It is in this context that the role of the salesperson takes on its relevance. In the face of this complexity, our clients need clarification, simplification, but also to be challenged and to be reassured in order to establish the right purchasing priorities that are in line with their strategy.

This clarification focuses, above all, on their needs. In a world that is more and more interconnected, a large and growing number of actors are involved in the decision-making. The result is an explosion of diverse and divergent needs. Whether it be within a family, a team or a department, the needs of each must be listened to and taken into account. The object selected, the service retained or the solution chosen must serve the majority. In so-called global companies the result is elongated decisional time frames.

A simplification in the way we do business is needed. It is important to make the sales relationship fluid and agile.

The best coaching that you can offer your client is to, as a first step, help create options that they hadn't thought about before, open new perspectives and new paths to explore; then as a second step, accompany them in accepting and appropriating the changes that these new perspectives are likely to trigger.

It is therefore crucial to reassure your client all along the process, bringing him to make choices up to their final decision. The best way to make the process comfortable for the two parties is to "say what we do and do what we say". It is just as simple – and difficult – as that. By adopting this attitude, you reinforce their trust, and, with the mirror effect, you can enable them to adopt the same attitude toward you, which contributes to developing a virtuous collaborative circle. When the final decision is not in your favor, you must respect it, humbly thank him for giving you the opportunity to compete and to learn. The best way to learn in such a situation is to propose a Loss Review with the client and your team. Certain clients decline the proposition because they fear that you will question their decision, but if you show your interlocutor a sincere desire to learn from their feedback and the firm intention to improve what failed, they will accept. That could be beneficial for them the next time.

To help your client in a meaningful way in the clarification of their needs and in the creation of new options, you need to work on the nature of your communications (i.e. your questioning) and on the base of their challenge (i.e. their change).

The art of the humble inquiry

In his book, *Humble Inquiry*, Edgar Schein brought "the subtle art of questioning rather than talking" to its peak. Addressed to managers in the medical profession who are used to telling their employees what they think they must know, with the consequence of immediately killing any new or innovative idea, Schein recommends practicing a "humble inquiry". He defines it as "the art of making someone talk, asking questions that we do not know the answer to, in order to build a relationship based on curiosity and interest in the other person". Approaching sales in the spirit of Schein, we understand the importance of establishing sincere relationships based on trust and respect. This approach is powerful for developing a protective relationship environment for yourself, your team and your client (Schein, 2011, 2013).

I like this approach. It supports the mindset and numerous principles elaborated in this book. In particular, it allows you to become aware of how this type of communication goes against traditional sales communication. Too many sales people don't listen, talk too much, and are essentially making affirmations. Questioning is reduced to a minimum. This is based on the belief that by explaining things (the features and the advantages of their product or service, the weaknesses of the competition, etc.), that is to say, by addressing their rational intelligence the client is going to understand why they should buy the product or service proposed (and certainly not the one from the competition). This way of proceeding goes from clumsiness to arrogance. Obviously you need to explain why your product or service is excellent, to compare it to the competition, and show all the advantages, but only once your client is ready to listen to you and understand. The majority of the time spent with your client must be dedicated to inquiring and a minimum to making affirmations. The less you speak, the more your brain becomes available to listen better, to observe, analyze, refine new questions, summarize, synthesize, correlate answers between them, come up with ideas, etc. So stay humble, be quiet and listen.

One of my mentors, a lawyer by training, was an expert in the art of making his interlocutor talk. One evening, I brought him to dine with the director of a big European scientific center, who was also a renowned physicist. During the three hours of our time together, my mentor asked only a few questions and made only a few comments. They were so pertinent that they led the physicist to talk about European political science, to explain the strong links between his research center and the industries that supplied them with new technologies, to take us through the latest developments in particle physics and to conclude with an enthusiastic analysis of the areas that he would like a partnership with us. Afterwards I learned how much the director of the center had appreciated my mentor, his understanding of the center's challenges, his brilliant intelligence and his willingness to collaborate. Following that, the director became one of our best sponsors.

In addition to the fact that it allows you to glean a lot of information, letting your client talk has the value of letting them project the image that they have of themselves. Later, their memory will associate this projection with the meeting. And as in general it is good, you come out a winner.

The art of accompanying change

All acts of purchase bring about a change. The purchase of a house or a car in the private sphere, or the replacement of an obsolete product by its most recent version, the replacement of a product or service by a competitive product or service or the implementation of a new strategy in the professional sphere, are changes that impact to varying degrees your interlocutor, their budget, habits, team, department or overall company. In the same way, the sale becomes a disruptive act that provokes a change for your client. All change requires letting go of the present and taking a risk for the future. It is therefore normal that the sale comes up against resistance.

The best way to overcome this resistance is to let your client appropriate the necessity of this change, to support them as they become aware that this change is beneficial for them, their team or company, then help them identify the option or the solution that suits them, and finally, to make them autonomous in making their choice, that is to say, the purchasing act.

This approach is at the heart of my relational approach to sales. In line with the spirit of the Schein approach, it is based on Motivational Interviewing (MI), well known by medical professionals and therapists, which is a method developed in 1983 by William Miller and Stephen Rollnick to take care of patients whose low level of motivation is usually an obstacle to change (Miller & Rollnick, 2012). "The Motivational Interview is a form of collaborative guidance, centered on the person that aims to raise and reinforce the motivation for change". The first use of MI in the coaching of executives dates from 2003 (Piazza, 2011).

To my knowledge, MI applied in a sales context has not yet been studied by the academic world. And yet, its underlying philosophy and technique proves to be a powerful facilitator of a win-win relationship and a co-built partnership.

Here are the principles that I used in my own experience and which are structured through the prism of Miller and Rollnick (Olivier Piazza, 2011). During the sales process you need to take your client through four prerequisites for change, using an open questionnaire that aims to stimulate their awareness 1) of their *desire* for the change, 2) of their *capacity* to change, 3) the *reasons* and 4) the *needs* for this change. For example, the following questions:

1. What would you like? What would you like to do? If you didn't have any limitations, what would your ideal solution be?... will explain their desire.

2. What could you do? What can you ask your teams? What help can you ask from your hierarchy?... connecting it to their own capacity, to their feeling of personal efficiency, to their authority.

3. Why do you wish to change? What would the advantages of this new solution be? What are the benefits of this change?... highlight their reasons for wanting to change.

4. Why must you change? How important is this change for you, your family, your team, your company?... will indicate their need to change.

This type of inquiry leads your client to identify numerous blocking points and to develop their own way to overcome numerous personal, technical and internal obstacles that you are not necessarily aware of. The answers to these questions are not always easy to put a value on, to quantify. The use of a scale from 0 to 10 can be pertinent to evaluate, for example, their degree of confidence. Thus: "How confident are you about obtaining approval from your board of directors? On a scale starting at 0, total absence of confidence, to 10, total confidence, where do you see yourself?" Not only does the answer provide you with valuable indications about the influence of their authority or the position expected from the board of directors, but it also allows you to follow up with more incisive questions for example: "Why are you at… and not at 0?" or "What is needed for you to pass from… to 10?". The use of the value scale also certainly applies to other elements that are a part of the sales process: aligning the solution to the needs of the client, the importance of the change, capacity to get resources, capacity to decide by which date, etc.

Next comes the choosing phase. Questions such as: "Where are you at in terms of your decision? What do you plan to do?" will indicate to you the degree of their *commitment* to the status quo or toward the change. It is common in sales to list and present the advantages of our solution. In fact, you can help them make a decision by using an alternative that is even more complete and subtle than this list. This approach is called "The Decisional Balance".

Status Quo		Option 1	
Pros	**Cons**	**Pros**	**Cons**
For me For my team For my company	For me For my team For my company	For me For my team For my company	For me For my team For my company
DECISIONAL BALANCE			

Instead of presenting them with your own point of view, ask your client to use a table with four columns and to begin by listing the advantages and disadvantages of the status quo in the first two. It's better to start there, in order to avoid raising resistance. Then have them list the advantages and disadvantages of the change that are linked to your solution in the last two columns. Have them itemize these points by taking their needs and wants into account on one hand (i.e. their authority, objectives, budget...) and their ecosystem on the other hand (i.e. their teams, colleagues, hierarchy, shareholders...). If you have created a sufficient alliance with your interlocutor, you can even filter these questions through their three spaces: intellectual, emotional and behavioral. This simple exercise allows your client to clarify their alternatives and expectations in-depth and allows you to better understand where you are in terms of their acceptance of your solution. Furthermore, proceeding as such respects the autonomy of your client and shows them that you respect them. For the client, the feeling of keeping control of their decision is an element of trust in their salesperson that prepares them to move forward.

Finally, it moves things into action. "How would you like to proceed?" Which steps do you recommend to reach an agreement?" make your client an actor in and responsible for their purchasing decision. When their propositions take time to be submitted, you can encourage them by using the hypothetical change: "Let's assume that you succeeded in convincing your board of directors, what could have made things possible?"

Of course, during these steps, you must juggle with your client's resistance. You will thereby avoid a hard confrontation with them, preferring attention, silence, reformulation and reframing. Remain humble. Work on the principle that a strong resistance on the part of your client is the result of your attitude being wrong. It is the sign that you must change it. No matter what is your point of view, your argument or your behavior. Also be convinced that a solution exists and that your client has it within them, which is the importance of the Motivational Interview which serves to "make it come out", to shape it and to actualize it. Thus it opens a creative space to co-build the best solution together. Your client has in them, their team, their business, the vast majority of the elements necessary for the design of the solution. It is up to you to assemble and fill in the puzzle with them. Finally, this inquiry also serves to reassure your client about their capacity to manage the change that this solution will lead to.

A phrase summarizes my approach: "Help me to help you".

Key take-aways

- Establish the Alliance with your client by associating the three components of trust (sincerity, respect, empathy) with a joint project

- Consider the sale as an opportunity (and a risk) of change for your client, their team and their company

- Be humble, ask your question, then be silent and listen

- Practice the Motivational Interview to help them change and purchase

- Use the 0 to 10 scale to measure a change

- Use the Decisional Balance to help them choose

- Ask them to help you to help them

CHAPTER 6

YOU ARE THE BOSS!

Understanding your role and determining what resources you have to reach your objectives is at the heart of your success. To do this, let's examine your ecosystem more closely. Take a sheet of paper, put your name at the center of it and divide the paper into four quadrants pointing toward the North, East, South and West, as shown in the illustration below.

U R the Boss !

The North indicates the members of your management, meaning, your direct hierarchy up to the highest level in the company, as well as your mentor(s).

The East names your colleagues, in particular your "advisors", those that are close to you, with whom you can test ideas, practice presentations or product demonstrations, role playing…

The South lists members of your team. This is composed of colleagues that you are not necessarily directly responsible for, but who get involved in collaborations with you on projects that you supervise. Your team also includes business partners outside of your company that collaborate with you or your team on your sales projects.

The West indicates your clients, and for each of them shows those who "make the decisions" those who "take the decisions" and those who are your sponsors. The West also indicates the clients of your clients with whom you can potentially be in contact. Understanding their needs helps a lot in proposing relevant solutions to your own clients.

This ecosystem presents all of the resources at your disposal that you can activate to build solutions that meet the needs of your clients, to obtain the necessary support as much internally, from your hierarchy, as externally, from your sponsors, and to challenge your ideas with your advisors or mentors.

The Jazz Team

No matter what position we have, we share our time between being an expert, a manager and a leader. That is to say between doing, having done, and inspiring to do. Depending on the activity and the degree of responsibility that we have we will be more involved in one of these three roles.

The most beautiful image I have to illustrate a top performing team is that of the "jazz team". In such a team, even if there is an official leader, the leadership circulates from one member to another depending on the development of the situation. Each of the members will be under the spotlight alternatively. They will be the star of the moment, while the others will accompany them in the shadows. Then the spotlight will move and light up another member of the team whose turn it will be to take the lead. Such a team works perfectly, displays a maximum of synergy, and uses the full complementarity of each one thanks to each member alternating between driving.

The Jazz Team

You are at the heart of this ecosystem. Your role will revolve around three modes: leader, facilitator, and performer.

As leader of the team, you will need to set the pace, meaning the rhythm at which the actions will be carried out to reach the objective in time. It is up to you to accelerate the speed within your organization and within your client's company when things start running late, and keep the dynamic going when things advance well.

As facilitator, you will compose the partition with your team and your client's team. You will ensure that each one contributes to the best of their abilities, the good synchronization of the teams involved to develop the messages together that make sense and resonate with the needs of your clients, to collaborate with the managers of the sectors involved, to correctly staff your teams and eliminate all obstacles to the positive conclusion of the sale. Just like in curling, you will make sure that you remove all the rough patches so that the rock arrives delicately in the middle of the target.

As a performer, you will play an instrument that is specific to you and differentiates you from the others in the action. For example, you will have a privileged relationship with certain members of management and you will open doors that, without you, would remain closed to your company. Another example is given by your capacity to activate the right people within your own company. This presumes a capacity to move with ease among your colleagues and the hierarchy of other units. A third example could be your capacity to find ingenious financial models offering multiple options and a flexible structure simplifying the way of doing business with your company.

In the role of orchestra conductor, it will be up to you to:

Inspire:

- trust
- the desire to do business with your company
- the desire to work with you

Drive:

- multidisciplinary teams

- negotiation teams

- the project management committee

Strengthen:

- synergy between your teams and your client's teams

- expertise and skills of your colleagues

- your network within your company, your client's company and externally

Be the guardian of the pace

One of the major responsibilities of the orchestra conductor is to ensure that everyone respects the pace. As all members of the orchestra start and finish at the same time, it is clear that they must be synchronized. It is up to you to ensure that this synchronization takes place internally, at your client and between the two teams. Clear and precise communication will facilitate the follow up of the collaboration process. Controlled and recognized leadership will allow you to reframe the phases of the sales process, to ensure the pace is respected and concludes in time.

Identify your resources, use them and take care of them

In such an ecosystem the resources that you have are rich, varied and numerous. It is crucial to realize that your own management and all of your hierarchy, up to the highest level of your company, are part of your resources. This reservoir of managers and executives, in principle, highly skilled, is there to help you, support you, bring their own added value and contribute to making the difference with the competition. It is useful and logical to get the members of senior management of your client in front of those of your own senior management. In addition to sensitizing your hierarchy to the reality of the field and the market, these encounters allow the passing of messages of which this hierarchy has the substance and control. For you, these encounters offer you a fantastic opportunity to learn. If you don't know who to get involved, ask your mentor or have them get involved.

Your client is also part of your resources. As we have seen, it is essential for you to have created a strong alliance with a small number of executives, or key interlocutors, that constitute the circle of your sponsors. Of course they begin, above all, with the idea of defending their interests and those of their company. Starting from the moment they are convinced that your actions will contribute to accompany in this direction, they will help you advance, slow you down if necessary and guide you in the right direction.

The other resources that you can count on from your client are their own experts. They love to talk about their profession, point out challenges, perspectives, the riches and they easily share their expertise. You just need to show an interest in others and their profession for them to tell you how they work. These technical teams are often the most available. Another category of experts that I often collaborate with is legal advisors. There is nothing like working together on the writing of big contracts to understand the culture, the operation, the politics and the skills of your client. When you work together several hours a day, several days per week, over a period of months, strong links are created that ensure the longevity of the partnership over the long-term.

As previously mentioned, the clients of your client are a very rich source of inspiration for developing solutions tailored to the market of your own client. In addition, once your clients' clients understand the advantages in helping you, they are open to providing you with information that, in the end, benefits them. One of my clients integrated standard electronic components to manufacture set-top boxes for his clients: French and British television companies. By understanding the features that these media companies might require in coming years, my team could even influence a more customized development of electronic components to propose to our integrator client. By understanding the advantage of our approach to their own needs, the French and British television companies welcomed our engineers for several months. The components that we developed afterwards corresponded exactly to their needs, which allowed us to win several contracts with our integrator client.

It is clear that the resources necessary to develop the solution to propose are to be cared for. They are those that, to a large extent, will make you reach, or not, your sales objective. Which is why it is so important to work in teams. This quality is not given to everyone. It requires work, patience and is built over time. The sales world consists mainly of individuals motivated by their own objectives, which does not always facilitate a team spirit. This is why it is essential to understand that it is misleading to think that one can succeed alone. That is relevant for a team, a unit, a company or a country.

The spirit of the "jazz team" that I spoke about facilitates this team synergy. It enhances it, creates the bond and allows each member to appropriate the meaning of the objective, on the condition that it was clearly communicated. It is remarkable to realize that by indicating the summit of the mountain to climb, the team manages to find the road, even if the leader has no idea how to get there. In fact, it is quite common to hear "The role of a leader is to get ordinary people to do extraordinary things". It is fascinating to see how a unified team starts to swing and improvise with brilliance when each one trusts the other, earning a standing ovation from the audience in the end, that is to say, from your client.

Thus, for each sales opportunity, your team will be composed of different members from each of the four quadrants. This team will be refreshed at each opportunity, with new participants ready to play a new partition under your direction as orchestra conductor.

You may also want to call upon resources that are outside of your professional ecosystem but which are very valuable and kind such as professional coaches, your family or your friends.

Certain companies have a pool of internal coaches or they may call external coaches. Make inquiries and use this option if it is available. You can also call an independent professional coach, on the condition that they are certified, they know the world of business, and they have a supervisor themselves. This requirement is misunderstood and often disregarded. However, it is the guarantor for you that your coach will have the guardrails necessary for a controlled and ethical practice.

Beginning at a certain age, let's say 35, it can be interesting to take a "reverse mentor". That is to say, a young professional for whom you will act as a mentor and who, in return, will be your mentor for new technologies, better use of social networks, the trends in culture, the arts, sports…

Finally, your family and friends are valuable sources of help and support. A very useful exercise consists of explaining in less than three minutes a concept, a product or a method to someone in your close circle who knows nothing about it. You see right away if what you are talking about is impactful, inspiring, makes sense … or is to be thrown out.

Master your elevator pitch

This exercise is called "The Elevator Pitch". It must be brief and convincing. It consists of communicating your message in a few minutes, the time that it takes an elevator to reach the top of a New York skyscraper.

The IT director of a big Swiss pharmaceutical company, with whom I was going to have lunch, told me about 50 meters before arriving to the restaurant: "my assistant informed me that you were working with him on a new business model concerning our sales relationship in Asia. You have until we reach the restaurant to explain the essence of what it's about". I didn't expect that, but the close collaboration with his teams prepared me well, I had the plan clear in my head and he appreciated my answer.

This type of request can happen at any moment. An efficient way to reply is to prepare a brief "elevator pitch" on each important subject in your field. This habit obliges you to examine these subjects yourself, to develop your own idea, to retain what makes sense for you and your clients. It makes your presentation more sincere and contributes to your credibility. Finally, use your elevator pitch as soon as you have the opportunity. The more that you share it, the more you receive feedback, the more you can refine it. As such, over time it will improve, become more pertinent and above all have more impact.

Master your communication

First and foremost, there are two golden rules to respect when you are operating at the heart of your ecosystem:

- *Vis-à-vis* your hierarchy, do not explain why something can't work. Explain what needs to be done for it to work. For example, don't say that you can't do your propositions because you don't have sufficient resources. Say rather: "To win this project, I need an architect, three specialists and a project manager".

- *Vis-à-vis* your team, you can delegate actions, but not the responsibility.

Within your ecosystem, you will be communicating with:

- your clients

- your management

- your colleagues

- your team

The fundamentals and the rules of good communication are the same for these four groups.

We will first address interpersonal communication then public communication. Good interpersonal communication (one to one) is based on three points:

1. Mastery of the language of the exchange. This point seems obvious, but must not be underestimated in the legal field where the writing of contracts requires a total mastery of the language of the exchange.

2. Mastery of writing. Writing notes without spelling mistakes, which are short, precise and easy to understand assures courteousness, respect and efficiency. Especially since emails are often sent to people that are not necessarily aware of the history. This habit will help you and your interlocutors gain time.

3. Mastery of the interview that is demonstrated through:

   - your speech flow

   - the clarity of your remarks

   - your silence

   - your visual contact

   - your gestures: the way you sit, eat, walk…

• your physical presentation: shaving, hair, odors, dress…

Here are a few rules to respect:

• Interact in mode adult–adult. This presumes on your part that your interlocutor and you are equals. You are not there to give lessons or to receive them. Nor is your interlocutor.

• Identify if you are dealing with an interlocutor that is an auditory or visual type. If you are addressing an auditory interlocutor focus on words, providing them with written elements and leaving them the time to listen again to what you have said or read what you have written. In the case of a visual interlocutor, use diagrams, and refer to mental images when you talk to them. It is important that you know yourself if you are more auditory or visual, for example if you prefer to have something explained with a lot of details, or if you prefer to look at a map. The knowledge of your own way of functioning allows you to either communicate in the same "language" as your interlocutor or to "translate".

• Be clear, concise and sober. The less that you speak, the more you will be heard. And the less that you speak, the more you will listen.

• Keep your partner informed regularly on the progress of the project in negotiation or in the process of deployment, even – and especially – if there is not any progress!

- Say what you do. Do what you say. This principle is proof of sincerity and reinforces trust.

- Put everything in writing: agenda, feedback, reports… On one hand, words spoken may be forgotten, words written remain. On the other hand, writing allows you to structure and specify your thoughts, to summarize and to keep track, put everyone on the same level of information, highlight the discrepancies, and progressively advance toward the final agreement.

- Say thank you. The best is to do so in writing. A very simple "thank you" will do.

My colleague David has a nice way of speaking about his relationships with his clients: "All interaction with your client is a unique and precious moment. It is a moment of truth".

Good presentation/communication in public (one to many) is based on four points:

1. Mastery of the language of the exchange.

2. Mastery of body language and the voice. Sixty per cent of the message is delivered through gestures and visual contact, 30% by voice and tone. Finally, 10% by the content. You can know your subject like the back of your hand or have learned your text by heart, but it is the expression on your face, your look, the use of your hands, your centered and assured posture and the controlled fluctuations in your voice that will trigger an emotion and touch your audience.

Even if an audience of scientists or engineers will concentrate more on the content than an audience of salespeople, they are all sensitive to the sincerity and the emotion conveyed by gestures and the voice.

The best way to prepare yourself to give a speech in public is to film yourself three times. For a presentation of about 20 minutes, this will require about an hour and a half. The result is impressive. The first recording will immediately show you everything that isn't right: stammering, jacket unbuttoned, not knowing what to do with your hands – above all do not put them in your pockets! The second recording will show that 80% of the faults in the first one were naturally corrected. It will allow you to position your voice, control what you do with your hands, and assert your posture. The third recording will show that you have mastered 80% of what was missing the second time. At this stage you will have mastered 96% of your speech in an hour and a half. The remaining 4% will leave room for improvisation and will make your speech more natural. For an investment of an hour and a half, it is really worth it.

3. The use of diagrams and texts. Your audience is a mix of people who are visual and auditory. You must make yourself understood by these two categories, which is why you need to alternate between diagrams or images and text.

4. **KISS**, or Keep It Simple, Stupid! Unless you are a specialist speaking to specialists on a specific subject, you will most often address people that, for the most part, don't know about what you are going to present to them. Without being too simplistic, your audience must easily understand things, not be drowned in jargon or pointless figures. Nicolas Boileau, French poet and writer, said in 1674: "Whatever is well conceived is clearly said, and the words to say it flow with ease". Apply this motto and everyone will thank you.

Be a humble leader

As we have seen, you have numerous resources to reach your objectives. It is up to you to know how to orchestrate them, to set them in motion at the right moment, in the most pertinent and harmonious way and at the right pace, to refer back to the image of the Jazz Team. In order to bring the others to success, three qualities will help you in your role as leader: sincerity, clarity and humility.

Being sincere brings you "to say what you believe in and believe in what you say". Your sincerity is even stronger when it is also based on coherence, a congruence between what you say and what you do. This attitude is the guarantor of your credibility.

Being clear in the definition of your objectives, your strategy and your roadmap, and communicating them in a simple, direct and understandable way, will ensure good communication.

Adopting a humble attitude within your team works in the same way as with your clients. It is about accepting that you can't control everything, to let go at certain times in order to better straighten things out at others, to call upon your colleagues that are more experienced or skilled than you in their field. It is the guarantor for mastering your Ego.

Finally, when we are surrounded by uncertainty, and we don't have all the information we wanted or wished to have to make the best choice, it can be tempting to not decide, or rather to decide to maintain the status quo and postpone a possible review of this decision for later on. This is sometimes a wise decision. Another approach is to establish an objective while being aware that it will probably be adjusted according to events that are, for the moment, unknown and state this fact clearly. While recognizing that you don't control everything, point a beam of light in the middle of the night and give a reference direction that you and those that accompany you can use as a guide. This kind of attitude reflects determination and flexibility. The reference direction allows you to measure and understand the deviation as the events take place. Thus, you reassure by reducing anxiety, stimulate action by avoiding inertia and focus efforts by eliminating dispersal.

Assure good follow-up

By saying what you do and doing what you say, you communicate in advance what you are going to do and afterwards you assure the follow-up of what you said.

Good follow-up is based on:

- regular contact, at a determined frequency

- thorough feedback

- a written summary

Depending on the hierarchy of your interlocutor, choose a weekly, monthly, quarterly, biannual or annual contact frequency. It is important to respect the frequency of these meetings, whether it be by phone or in person.

A weekly contact with your hierarchy, even brief, is necessary. This can be done by phone, in person or in writing. For the follow-up of important projects a written summary is essential and, in certain cases, will be daily. Certain critical situations require constant follow-up made possible by the instantaneousness and increase in our means of communications.

Keeping your colleagues and your teams informed guarantees good team work and their implication in what you do. Depending on the implication of your teams, a regular update will allow you to communicate about what took place, what is taking place, and what you would like in the future. This way of operating assures an alignment of resources that you need for projects that are underway or to start soon. These meetings allow the teams to not only know where you want to go but also to prepare according to their own constraints, availability and skills.

Finally, good follow-up respects three rules:

- anticipate requests

- communicate regularly

- don't leave things waiting

If you don't have the information requested or the proposition expected by your client, if the delivery is late, call your client proactively, keep them informed about the situation and inform them of what you are doing to correct the situation. They will see that, even if things are not as they wished, or expected, they are progressing. These three rules are reassuring and reinforce trust.

How to get help

We have seen the importance of teamwork. More specifically, how are you going to get help?

First of all, by working with your partner: they could be a specialist in your team, another salesperson, your direct manager… they must be able to challenge you, complete you, replace you when you are absent, know the file, the project and be impacted by the result of the sale. This last point is a critical perquisite for them to be totally committed.

Then, leverage your ecosystem, a phenomenal reservoir of resources. Getting help requires you to act quickly, with no delay, as soon as you sense the need for help. Do not hesitate to ask for help as there is nothing wrong with this. It's a sign of clear thinking and intelligence. You don't necessarily have the time to do everything, you don't have the answer for everything and you are not skilled in everything. It's a fact. Clarifying a point, challenging an idea, getting help with a tool that you don't master, will make you gain time, enrich your knowledge and your know-how, and increase the added value for the client. Your objective is to win. All that can contribute to increasing this added value and to reaching your objective is legitimate and must be put in place.

Clearly establish the issue that you are seeking help for and, if possible, do so in writing. You cannot allow yourself to lose time going back and forth, or to lose time for the person you are seeking assistance from.

Before asking for help, define what you need by reviewing the tools you have to negotiate:

- Is my strategy clear?

- What is the primary innovation topic of my long-term strategy?

- Who is my client's sponsor within my hierarchy?

- What are my main strengths? My assets?

- Who is my partner?

- Is my Elevator Pitch on my subject, my strategy, my products or my services sufficiently developed and refined?

Coordinate the follow-up of your requests. In a sales project, you must pay attention to many things and sometimes you will be making several requests for help at the same time.

By assuring the follow-up of your requests you will avoid delays, stress, last-minute refusals or even blocking of the project.

How to manage your management

Your management's role and mission is, essentially, to support you (in the development of your skills, your motivation, your career, with changes in the organization, in your sales approach toward your clients, in your teamwork with your colleagues…), to supervise you (*vis-à-vis* respecting company rules, business ethics, or following the sales process) and to measure you (your performance progress, reaching your objectives). These three actions are valid regardless of the type of company, its size or business sector. So how can you intelligently get along with your hierarchy?

The first thing you must determine is: what does your manager expect from you? Having led very diverse teams for many years, there were two fundamental principles that I wanted my sales teams to respect. The first is what I call the reality principle, and the second is the reliability principle.

The reality principle is your ability to perceive reality as it is: to understand what is behind your client's words. To grasp the meaning of things left unsaid and the impact they have on the negotiations, to know how to interpret behavior and be sure of your interpretations, to evaluate the chances of the sale happening, are a few examples of what you must know how to decipher correctly in order to be realistic.

The reliability principle is your ability to understand and explain reality as honestly as possible. Lying knowingly, hiding the truth thinking that the problems will resolve themselves, in fear of having to admit a weakness, a difficulty or a mistake, or worried about displeasing your hierarchy, are behaviors to be banned. On the contrary, saying what you think about the situation, about what needs to be done to win, and in the most precise, complete and honest way possible, increases your manager's trust in you. Respecting these two principles reassures your manager about your analytical ability and the trust that you deserve. They can rely on your judgment and count on you.

I established ten rules of managerial cooperation that will allow you to work intelligently with your hierarchy:

1. Know how your manager works in terms of their emotions, mindset and behavior.

2. Know your manager's priorities and help them to achieve them.

3. Know their rules of the game – and accept them.

4. Keep your manager informed regularly, before they ask you.

5. Avoid surprises at all costs: good ones as much as bad ones, because it can give the impression that you don't have things under control or that you are not able to anticipate.

6. Don't just come with problems, but bring suggestions and/or solutions.

7. Ask for and give feedback (in an adult-to-adult mode).

8. Help your manager help you. To do this, tell them what you need.

9. Keep your promises.

10. Bring the main members of your hierarchy with you to your client. This will show them the reality of the field, get them out of their sphere, show them how you manage the relationship with the client and give them the opportunity to add value, which will allow you to learn from them.

Go back over the elements of this paragraph and ask yourself the question:

What can I do to improve the way I communicate, whether it be face-to-face, in public, with my colleagues and my team, with my management or with my client?

Key take-aways

- Identify the ecosystem that you "conduct"

- Lead a Jazz Team

- Use your Mentor and your Reverse Mentor

- Master your Elevator Pitch

- Remember that your message is communicated, above all, non-verbally

- Be clear and concise

- Say thank you

- Manage your management

- Know how to get help

CHAPTER 7

IF YOU WANT TO GO FAR, TAKE CARE OF YOUR HORSE

When we fly in an airplane, just before takeoff, the steward asks us to fasten our seatbelt before helping fasten our children's, the very ones we care the most about. This request is full of good sense. The rule applies to any situation in your life: you must first take care of yourself in order to be able to take care of others.

I always say that the person you must "support" the longest is yourself. In English, support means to give help or assistance, while in French it means to endure or tolerate. Here I use the word first in the French sense, linked to the duration and then move toward the English version, linked to assistance.

To have to support yourself all of your life is the main reason that it is in your interest to love yourself and to take care of yourself. This seems obvious but not many people actually do it. In particular, energetic salespeople with a fast-paced life, overwhelmed by their objectives and living under the dictatorship of their quota. Loving yourself and taking care of yourself allows you to reach your full potential.

Love yourself with clear thinking, kindness and support

To be able to understand and master things, you have to start by learning. Learning consists of observing, practicing and concentrating. The more you practice, the better you concentrate and the better you can do what you are trying to do. It is the famous four-phase spiral of developing a skill, such as driving for example. At first, you don't know what you don't know how to do; then you become aware of what you don't know how to do (break and shift the clutch at the same time, hold the steering wheel correctly while looking in the rear-view mirror); then you become fully aware of what you know how to do (parallel park well, apply the driving rules); and finally, you become unconscious of what you know how to do (to the point that you don't remember which route you took). However, this last phase is like being on "automatic pilot" which, in reality, is counterproductive to "doing well". For example, it gives you the illusion that you can do something else at the same time as driving, such as being on the telephone, with consequences that can be, at times, dramatic.

Control consists of being fully aware of what you are doing. This assumes that you are highly concentrated on the action in progress thanks to an ability to let distraction pass by and remain focused calmly on what you are in the process of doing.

Self-development is a source of serenity. The command that you gain of your mind, your body, your abilities, your skills, your behavior and your emotions, gradually builds confidence in yourself then the certainty that you can count on yourself. This control and confidence makes you serene.

Control, confidence and serenity are contagious. They inspire others. They show that *savoir, savoir-faire* and *savoir-être* are possible, and thus accessible. They motivate others to want to do the same, each in their own sphere. The control with which you carry out an activity, whatever it may be, the confidence that you express and the serenity that exudes from you, ensures that you will become a role model. Being a role model can happen with your family, a community, your team or your clients.

Loving yourself will allow you to believe in yourself, in your abilities and your possibilities. It's not a narcissistic love, according to which you would be the most attractive, the most intelligent, etc. Narcissistic love, driven by this Ego whose misdeeds we have already outlined several times, is detrimental and handicapping because it absorbs your energy by focusing it on you, instead of focusing it on what must be done for you and for others. The love of oneself that I am talking about is clear, kind and supportive. Thanks to its clarity, you see yourself as you are. Its kindness makes you accept yourself as you are. Its support makes you believe in yourself and thus motivates you to develop yourself.

Combining clarity and kindness makes you understand and accept your imperfections, but also understand and accept those of others. Clarity and kindness help us develop our humility. As we have already observed, humility is not resignation. Humility is the awareness and acceptance that the world is not perfect. However, humility does not keep us from taking action, while resignation is the belief that we cannot change the situation in any way.

Clarity and support are precious aides for becoming aware and deciding which qualities, skills and habits should be maintained, developed or reinforced, and which faults, weaknesses and habits are to be corrected, abandoned or overcome.

Finally, kindness and support are powerful stimulants for developing and improving what is good for you over the long-term. They help you accept the fact that success is full of many falls from which they will help you rise.

Optimizing your own development makes you available to help others, and credible to be a role model. The openness and kindness that you demonstrate for yourself will help you do so for others. Your awareness of your imperfection will contribute to your accepting that of others. Not only will it slow down your impatience when you feel as though others are progressing and changing slowly, but it will also make you accept more easily that others don't want to change.

Take care of you

Taking care of yourself is essential to becoming a successful salesperson and remaining one. You need to put in place a sales hygiene that is based on the trio of physical, mental and emotional hygiene.

Physical hygiene

By physical hygiene I mean taking care of your "physical infrastructure", that is your body and its metabolism. It is based on sleep, diet, physical exercise and an annual medical checkup.

a. *Respect your sleep*

If your sleep is disrupted, all the rest becomes disrupted; you lack energy, your enthusiasm goes down, fatigue sets in, irritability increases, you lose confidence and your sleep becomes even more unsettled. On the other hand, good sleep allows you to recharge your batteries, keep your energy intact, manage your stress and reinforce your immune system. In fact, more than respecting it, you need to take care of your sleep, pamper it, and make it your friend. A healthy, undisrupted night's sleep is the first ally of a salesperson.

Salespeople are often victims of sleep disorders that range from a few nocturnal wakings to severe insomnia. These disorders can originate from various sources and you must consult a doctor to determine the specific cause and the appropriate treatment. In certain cases, it comes from a poor quality of life caused by harmful habits linked to the inappropriate use of our mobile phones, tablets and other portable devices common in the life of a salesperson. This is why I am going to share with you how I successfully treated insomnia thanks to six simple rules from cognitive-behavioral therapy techniques. My point in using this example is to help you become aware of how a few disciplined good habits can change your life and open you to a new sense of wellbeing. The rules are simple and the method's only constraint is the discipline with which they must imperatively be applied.

- **Rule No. 1:** Wake up at the same time each day, including weekends and holidays. For example at 6:30 am.

- **Rule No. 2:** Determine the number of hours that seem optimum for a restful sleep (for example, seven and a half hours) and go to bed at the appropriate time (e.g. 11:00 pm).

- **Rule No. 3:** Don't use multimedia devices (computer, tablet, mobile phone, TV or cinema) one hour before going to bed, that is to say, starting at 10:00 pm. This is because the light from screens disturbs your production of melatonin and keeps you awake. It is one of our adolescents' major problems.

- **Rule No. 4:** Put in place a bedtime routine, fifteen to twenty minutes before going to bed. For some people, this brings to mind childhood stories, but for adults there are more choices: there is indeed the choice of reading a light book or a simple magazine, taking a shower, using lukewarm or cold water to lower body temperature, drinking relaxing herbal tea, practicing mindfulness meditation which soothes our mind or having a cuddle that releases endorphins. Depending on the amorous phase you are going through, meditation is perhaps the most restful.

- **Rule No. 5:** In the case of a nocturnal waking, even a very light one, do not look at your alarm clock. Knowing what time it is can keep you from going back to sleep, either because it is the middle of the night and you might become anxious, or because there is less than an hour left before it's time to get up and you're not going to be able to go back to sleep.

- **Rule No. 6:** In the case of a prolonged waking in the middle of the night, you must not stay in bed: go sit in a comfortable chair and look through a magazine with a soft light.

Keep a sleep journal for a month to help you put these rules in place and reinforce your motivation: by noting each day the number of hours of sleep and wake time from the night before, the number of nocturnal wakings and possible fatigue of the current day, you follow the progress of improvements achieved.

Why do these simple rules work well? Because they reprogram your brain to consider your bed for what it is: a place of rest. When we are hungry and we see food, we drool. When a good sleeper is tired and goes to bed, they fall asleep right away. Their brain knows that the bed will provide them the rest that they need. These rules worked perfectly for me. They required pretty radical changes in my logistics and habits, in particular the rule that forbids the use of multimedia devices. But they changed my life: I now wake up early, which gives me the feeling of having more control over my day. I no longer fear a bad night because I know that I have a method that suits me well. These rules got me back to "slowing down": by eliminating the aggressiveness of a screen light, the restlessness of internet research, the overload of information from the latest news or the excitement of a movie, they forced me to turn to activities that are more laid back, relaxing or reflective. And my brain relearned what a bed is.

b. *Respect your diet*

Obesity has become a national health problem in Western countries and it is developing rapidly in emerging countries. Most people who would like to be careful about what they eat look to special diets. That is to say, methods that tell you what you should eat, how much and when to eat it. Unfortunately these approaches don't work because they are based on an intellectualization of food by disconnecting the real needs of the person who is eating. Almost all of the diets recommended for the last thirty years result in failure. People that followed them gained back more than they lost. It is the notorious yo-yo effect, which over time, confuses the body, increases the level of fat in the blood, and creates a nagging frustration and loss of self-confidence.

An approach that ensures that you will eat correctly over the long-term is one that is centered not on the food, but on the person eating the food. This approach, also from cognitive-behavioral therapy, is also based on a few simple rules and requires great discipline. Yet, these rules are naturally practiced by those who don't have a weight problem. Over a lifetime, the weight of such people only varies by a few kilos, while someone living in the West, eating on average 1.5 kg of food per day, for eighty years, consumes 44 tons of food over their lifetime. This shows that our body is a machine capable of remarkable self-control when we don't disrupt it.

- **Rule No. 1:** Only eat when you are hungry.

- **Rule No. 2:** Stop eating when you are no longer hungry.

- **Rule No. 3:** Chew each mouthful for at least ten seconds.

- **Rule No. 4:** Wait at least ten seconds before taking another mouthful.

- **Rule No. 5:** Make sure that the meal lasts at least twenty minutes.

- **Rule No. 6:** Don't do anything except eat. Don't read, don't listen to the radio, and especially don't watch television. Concentrate on what you are eating in order to avoid taking in the food automatically, in particular when you are sharing a meal with friends. Savor and enjoy the taste of food; eat mindfully.

These rules appear to be simple, and yet they are difficult to follow for someone who unlearned how to eat correctly for many years. Everything around us pushes us to break these rules: we eat quickly, in just a few minutes, we swallow food that is increasingly liquid, too sugary or too salty, and we do several things while eating. A common aberration is the package of popcorn that many audiences eat automatically at the beginning of a movie. Rare are those who would devour the same amount of popcorn in a context other than the one conditioned by the cinema. In addition, more and more people are eating alone. Solitude, boredom, sadness and fatigue are contributing factors of "bad eating".

Rather than knowing if we need to stop eating this or that food, weighing quantities, avoiding this or that association of foods, in short complicating life, it's better to focus on the basics, according to these rules, to be able to keep the freedom of eating in a way that suits us and fits our metabolism. For people with pronounced excess weight, I advise adopting this approach with the support of a psychologist trained in cognitive behavioral therapy, and following a medical check-up. It is, in fact, harder to regulate weight than sleep by yourself because eating is linked to many genetic, emotional, psychological and behavioral factors whose interactions are complicated to untangle. This regulation takes time because you need to work on your buried emotions, limiting beliefs and compulsive behaviors. Self-observation is essential for doing this work. It is only with adequate support that you will be able to guide your own observations and emotions to draw conclusions and learn useful lessons.

It can seem unrealistic for some people to believe that these rules can be applied in the hectic, competitive, connected, digitalized world in which we live. This is a mistake. It is up to us to define our priorities, to determine what needs to be done and to give ourselves the means to do it.

The advantages and the benefits of this approach are numerous:

- You rediscover the taste of food.

- You experience the pleasure of savoring it.

- You enjoy a moment of calm at each meal.

- You rediscover the feeling of hunger and satiety.

- You are the actor of your own wellbeing.

- You become aware that you are doing something good for yourself.

- You realize that you have your own "medicine" in yourself.

- You lose weight progressively without frustration.

I put the loss of weight as the last point because, if it is often initially the priority objective, it becomes a natural consequence of all of the other results. If you consider yourself "gourmand", I strongly recommend this approach in order to become "gourmet".

c. *Respect your body*

This respect takes place by practicing a non-excessive physical activity on a regular basis. I am referring to a physical activity but not necessarily a sport. As the borderline can be a bit blurry, let's clarify: doing three to four hours per week of physical exercise in a gym or at home is considered regular physical activity and not excessive. Training to do a marathon is sport. Targeting to finish in first place is competition.

The first objective of practicing a physical activity is to keep our "machine" in good shape, as long as possible. The second is to enable it to develop and to progress. Everyone will find an activity that suits them, from a simple daily walk to martial arts. What matters is to do at least three to four hours of physical activity per week, spacing out the activity by at least 48 hours in order to let your muscles regenerate correctly and to avoid muscular or joint injuries.

In addition to this weekly physical activity, an excellent way to start your day is to do the "sun salutation" when you get up. It is a set of yoga postures that you can easily find on the internet.

A simple exercise for reinforcing balance, to be done after the sun salutation, consists of "doing the pink flamingo". Stand on one leg and bend the other one, putting your foot on the inside of the upright leg at the knee level. Place your hands on your waist. Balance yourself for 30 seconds, then do the exercise on the other leg. Over time, as your balance becomes easily maintained, prolong the duration of the exercise to one minute, then one and a half minutes, etc. up to three minutes. Then do the exercise for 30 seconds... with your eyes closed. Oh yes, it's a little bit harder!

Good balance develops progressively, naturally and without effort. The brain learns alone. This balance is based on "proprioception", from the Latin word *proprius* (i.e. proper) and (re)ception, referring to perception, conscious or not, of the different parts of the body thanks to numerous muscle and ligament receptors, tracts and nerve centers.

The benefits of this exercise are numerous. By concentrating on your body in a very specific way, proprioceptive balance enables you to start your day calmly and in tune with yourself. You measure your progress easily and daily, which gives you a strong feeling of self-control. Finally, it calls upon your own internal resources and thus strengthens your self-confidence.

Combining the sun salutation, which refreshes us, and the proprioceptive balance exercise, which settles us, takes 15 minutes maximum. This combination starts your day on a positive, serene and confident note.

Last but not least, it is important to have a medical check-up at least once a year. The best way to remember is to do it on your birthday. This check-up consists of a medical visit, a blood test and additional tests depending on your age and sex. These are the ABCs of prevention. They will help you avoid unpleasant surprises and reassure your hypochondriac side.

Mental hygiene

Just as there are rules for physical hygiene, positive psychology has shown, since the year 2000, based on numerous academic, scientific and rigorous works, that there are rules for mental hygiene, and that these rules can facilitate access to happiness.

Happiness is a bit like intelligence: it is difficult to define, but when we are in its presence, we recognize it. Christophe André, one of the best French specialists on happiness, told a journalist during a radio interview: "Happiness is wellbeing that we are conscious of". I like this definition, both simple and elegant.

It allows me to introduce here a traditional practice, known for a long time by many philosophical or religious schools, and one which the West is beginning to integrate a bit everywhere in society. That is, full consciousness. This practice consists of living in the present moment, no matter what activity you are doing, by becoming aware of what you feel, what you think and how you are acting in the moment. You can walk in full consciousness, eat in full consciousness, take a shower in full consciousness, or meditate in full consciousness. This type of meditation is developing under the name of *mindfulness meditation*.

The search for happiness has been a human quest since the beginning of time. According to Christophe André, when we feel good and we feel this wellbeing, recognize it and appreciate it at the moment that it happens, we experience happiness. This experience is, of course, ephemeral, but the more you get yourself in condition to experience it, the more you will feel this moment of happiness.

Neuroscience shows us that we possess the resources to achieve it. You don't need external objects or mood enhancing substances to be happy. Your brain, with its own endorphins, and your mind, with its willingness, are completely sufficient.

Some excellent works by renowned scientists and authors present the keys to learning how to build genuine happiness day after day. (Achor, 2011; Ben-Shahar, 2008, 2014: Boniwell, 2012, Hefferon & Boniwell, 2011, Lyubomirsky, 2013; Seligman, 2011).

To become a successful salesperson, three daily practices will help you develop strong mental power, unwavering confidence in yourself and positive self-esteem. These three practices are:

- Mindfulness meditation, for 15–30 min/day

- Writing, for 5 min/day

- Self-education, for 30 min/day

As you can see, this shouldn't take you more than one hour per day. Which is not a lot compared to the benefits that you will feel as soon as you put these practices into place.

a. Practice mindfulness meditation

I started to meditate in full consciousness several years ago thanks to the works of Dr. Jon Kabat-Zinn (2004, 2005). His methodical approach, devoid of spiritual or religious references, has been applied by numerous hospital centers and meditation groups for more than 30 years, with great success. I thought that if his approach prevents depression and relieves the suffering of severe illnesses, it could help me draw out my inner resources and activate defense mechanisms difficult to reach with sheer willingness.

The following exercise is a variation of the "body scan": easy to do, it will bring you strength and serenity. It lasts between 15 and 30 minutes and you can practice it at any time of the day. I recommend doing it in the morning, but you can use it in the evening to prepare for sleep, as we have addressed in the treatment of insomnia. It is also useful for creating a transition space for you between two very absorbing activities during the day. Each time you feel the need and time allows, practice it: like all the exercises presented in this book, repetition creates a routine and strengthens control.

The objective of this exercise is to let go of ideas that appear in your head. Imagine that the blue sky is your mind and the white or dark clouds are your ideas. As the exercise progresses, the clouds will appear: let them go by, watch them pass, don't hang on to them. Focus on the exercise. Concentrate on your breathing according to the following protocol:

- Find a calm spot where you will not be bothered for the duration of the exercise. Turn off your mobile phone.

- Sit in a chair with your feet flat on the ground, your back straight, good posture, your forearms placed on your thighs, your hands on your knees or one hand in the palm of the other.

- Close your eyes.

- Breathe in through your nose by releasing your diaphragm and inflating your stomach.

- While breathing in, feel the air that enters through your nostrils, and goes into your lungs. Imagine that this air continues to descend and goes toward your left foot. Visualize the air turning around in your foot, as if it was massaging it from the inside.

- Then, breathing out, visualize the air leaving your foot, which becomes a beautiful light that is soft and warm. The air goes up your leg, crosses your lungs and comes out your nostrils, or your mouth if you prefer.

- Breathe in again and proceed in the same way by visualizing the air going through the inside of the bottom of your left leg.

- Breathe out by letting your left leg transform into this beautiful warm and soft light, the air goes up, crossing your lungs before going out through your nostrils or your mouth.

- Repeat this alternation of inhaling and exhaling by visualizing the flux of air that goes into a place in your body, transform it into light and leaves.

- Proceed like this going all over your body: after the left leg, go to the right leg then to the pelvis, the rib cage, to your arms and your hands then your shoulders, your neck, face and finally to the top of your head.

- At that moment you have scanned all of your body, and it has progressively transformed into a beautiful warm and soothing light. Now all of your body is light. Savor its presence, its peacefulness, its permanence. Feel its warmth, energy and power.

- Calmly open your eyes and, little by little, reconnect with your body's movements.

The exercise is done. It lasted about 15 minutes. If you would like to prolong it you just need to increase the number of crossings through your body. As you will experience in doing it, the main difficulty is letting go of the multiple thoughts that appear and interfere with your breathing and moving you away. This is understandable because it is the intended goal: the objective is not to get rid of the thoughts, it is to let them go by. If this is more difficult for you at certain times than others, accept it, be kind with yourself, and gently bring your mind back to your breathing.

Its benefits are numerous. It provides you with a space for a daily meeting with yourself. It teaches you to let go and makes you aware that the thoughts are not the reality: they are just thoughts. Thanks to this perspective, it helps you to be lucid, serene and humble. Finally, for those who practice this type of meditation over the long-term, medical science has observed an improvement in cognitive, hormonal and immune functions.

b. *Write for three minutes per day*

The evening, before going to bed, take a moment to write the three things that made you happy that day. It could be the hint of a smile in meeting someone, the flight of a bird, a phone call to someone close, the running of a project, a client visit, etc. We have millions of opportunities to experience moments of joy, pleasure or happiness all day long.

This daily practice allows you to:

- Become aware that despite all the frustrations of the day, everything that couldn't get done, or that didn't work right, there were still *at least* three moments of happiness.

- Know that *tomorrow* there will also be three moments of happiness. Progressively, you will become more available to receive them, to savor them and make them last.

- Perceive that happiness can be found just as much in unique moments, linked to an event, a success or an exceptional encounter, as in the small moments, fleeting, simple and trivial. But as these are the most frequent, our happiness lies in great part in ordinary things.

- Finally, this brief writing is an excellent ritual for preparing to go to sleep.

c. Teach yourself every day

Continuous education has become an absolute necessity. If we want to stay up-to-date on developments in our industries, professions and technologies, we must learn, unlearn, and relearn constantly. The only way to do this is to take responsibility for our own education by using traditional courses and new learning methods made available through the internet.

The Web has revolutionized the content of knowledge that is now available as much as it has the way that we access it. No matter where we are we have access to an enormous amount of knowledge that mankind has never seen before, all just a simple click away.

But too much information kills knowledge. Which is why it is indispensable to make your own training plan each year. Establish the subjects that you would like to develop, the topics that you would like to learn and master and the companies (real or virtual) that can provide information on these subjects and the means to access it.

As a salesperson, there are three important areas in which you may need to increase your knowledge: the industry in which you work, the products or services that you sell and those of your competition, and your personal and interpersonal skills. These relational skills include those that Anglo-Saxons call "soft skills" and all the practices related to them.

In the same way as you eat an elephant bite by bite, solid education is acquired day by day. It is the principle of school, junior high, apprenticeship or university. It is up to you, in each of these three areas, to choose the subjects that you would like to work on, estimate the time period by which you want to master the chosen subject, and allocate a minimum of 30 minutes each day to the subject. In the case of complex subjects and/or ones that are long to learn, it can be useful to follow structured classes on the internet such as specialized webinars or Massive Open Online Courses (MOOC). These kinds of classes provide a framework with a structure, a plan, time frames and checkpoints.

However, education is not only acquired in a book or on the internet. An MBA hands you the concepts and the vocabulary of the business world on a silver platter, but it does not make you a manager. This book provides the elements for becoming an excellent salesperson but reading it isn't enough. Management or sales is like parachuting, it is not learned in books, but rather from practice in the field. Spend time learning from your clients, put yourself in a learning position by listening to them and observing them. Do the same with the best of your colleagues... and your competition. And tell yourself that the day you no longer learn, or you no longer admire anything, you are no longer alive.

Emotional hygiene

Here we address the most delicate subject, the one that bothers people: emotions. It is also the most misunderstood and ignored subject. For reasons linked to cultural and social protocols, to family and school education, to religion, and to company codes, it is difficult for most of us to recognize our emotions, express them, manage them and tame them.

Emotion comes from the Latin word *motio*, which means to set in motion. There are two ways to put yourself in motion: either in a proactive way, from a strength we have that pushes us to act, to put ourselves in action; or in a reactive way, in reaction to an external force that pushes us to react.

The emotions that set us in motion are numerous if one believes in the work of specialists (Sander & Scherer, 2014). Nevertheless, the four basic emotions are: joy, sadness, anger and fear. Some would add surprise, disgust and shame.

My purpose here is not to explain how these emotions work. It is to familiarize you with tools that allow you to manage them, in particular in the sales context.

a. Non-violent communication

We often believe that empathy is an innate quality. We have it or we don't. By participating in workshops on non-violent communication techniques (NVC) developed in the 1960s by Marshall Rosenberg, I realized that empathy can be developed in individuals that initially seem to be lacking it. By working on active listening, letting go and humility, these individuals were capable of being empathetic with other members of the groups after one day. After two days of the workshop, in many cases, the benefits for participants in their couple, family or professional relationships were visible and immediate.

By developing your empathy, this method makes you capable of stimulating the empathy of your interlocutor. It is therefore very powerful for establishing caring relationships while asserting yourself and making yourself respected, and, if necessary, stopping, without being aggressive and in a firm way, a malicious intrusion.

Marshall Rosenberg's NVC is based on three main elements:

- The recognition of your emotions

- A symmetry in the consideration of each person's emotions

- A protocol based on specific rules for managing conflict

Stating the rules of this protocol will allow you to understand the essence of the method without requiring additional explanations. If you would like to examine this exciting field further I recommend Marshall Rosenberg's wonderful book, *Nonviolent Communication: a Language of Life.*

- **Rule No. 1:** Start with a triggering fact.

It is essential that the triggering event is really a fact, and not an interpretation of a fact. For example, if you are verbally aggressed, you can start a non-violent communication by repeating what you heard: "I hear that you just said 'You are a liar' " and above all avoid: "If I understand well, you are calling me a liar". Your interlocutor cannot contest the exact sentence that they said, that you heard and you repeated, while they could deny your interpretation, which would quickly make the discussion get out of control.

- **Rule No. 2:** Express how you feel.

The same as someone cannot deny if you are thirsty or hungry, no one can deny if you feel sad, angry or tired.

For example, saying that: "hearing it stated that I am a liar hurts me deeply" cannot be contested. While saying: "saying that hurts me" puts the responsibility of your feelings on your interlocutor and leads them to come back with an argument.

- **Rule No. 3:** Invite your interlocutor to express how they feel.

By adopting this symmetrical attitude, you open a space for them of freedom and responsibility for their own feelings. At the same time, you adopt a caring position that will induce a mirror effect in them. This resonance is the beginning of mutual understanding and acceptance of each other. For example, continue the discussion by asking: "what fact leads you to say that to me?" and "how did you feel after this fact?" helps them express their emotions.

- **Rule No. 4:** Recognize their feeling and ask them to recognize yours.

This comes from an adult–adult approach and strengthens the symmetry of the exchange by placing your interlocutor on equal terms with you. Recognizing how someone else feels is a mark of respect and a characteristic of empathy. It soothes the other person and encourages them to do the same thing as you. Tension is reduced significantly. This posture invites dialogue.

- **Rule No. 5:** Find a solution together so that each person feels comfortable and the situation will not happen again.

Use the opening of the dialogue to explore resolution options together that would be acceptable for both and at the same time, long-lasting. Duration is a form of protection and a prerequisite for the solution to be chosen. Maintaining a position of equality between the two parties and using a kind and engaging tone allows each person to start to express themselves in a constructive way. Often, at this stage, things accelerate and ideas come more quickly than expected. After the storm, the sun suddenly appears.

- **Rule No. 6:** Agree on the concrete actions to be put in place.

When the two parties agree on the solution's principle, the actions are generally not numerous and are very easy to establish. Each person is happy to have found a solution and is eager to get through it!

Here is a real life situation in which I used this protocol with success. The context of the situation was as follows: one of my colleagues, the financial director of our division, had the habit of entering my office abruptly and without knocking. Authoritarian by nature, he acted the same way with everyone. This exasperated me and I decided to put an end to it by using NCV. The day that he started again, I applied the rules one after the other.

- I began with a fact – incontestable – that he didn't knock at the door and he entered brusquely.

- I told him that I had observed this fact several times and that "this brusque interruption startled me and physically disturbed me". I added that "it did not allow me to be in the right condition to listen to him with all the attention he deserved and that I wish to give to my interlocutors".

- I asked him why he acted in this way, what he felt at that moment, and let him speak. After a long silence, he uttered that he hadn't paid attention to his behavior, that he was often in a hurry and that he understood that this could bother me.

- Without adding anything on either side, we agreed that he would knock and that I would do my best to respond to his pressing issues.

- The incident was closed and a better ambience was established.

This example is trivial but still reflects the daily reality with its small quirks that end up poisoning office life. It's the same in a couple, with our children, our parents or our friends. In these contexts, NCV develops our self-assertion through respect that we consciously give to others and that we clearly ask to receive in return.

b. *Emotional Freedom Techniques (EFT)*

Emotional Freedom Techniques are simple healing methods that you can use either alone or with the help of a therapist. They combine the benefits of traditional so-called energy techniques, such as acupuncture, acupressure, shiatsu or kinesiology, with recent advances in neuro-linguistic programming and certain cognitive therapies that heal phobias. The techniques were developed by Gary Craig who, after having developed and refined them during the 1990s, generously shared them with the world by publishing them on the internet.

Simply, it is tapping a series of well-established meridian points while repeating kind statements about yourself that are linked to your emotional problem. This seems simplistic, even incongruous. Especially because no one knows exactly how it works. And yet the results are quick and spectacular.

Three years ago I participated in a workshop over a weekend given by my friend Jean-Michel Gurret, the first French therapist to have been certified as an EFT practitioner by Gary Craig. One of the participants was an older woman who had walked up stairs with great difficulty with the help of a cane, for many years. Before participating in an EFT session given by Jean-Michel in public, she explained to us that this situation had endured since the death of her husband and serious disagreements with her family. The next morning, she showed us, very happily, how she went up and down the staircase that led to the classroom without the help of her cane and without pain. We thought it was a prank, but Jean-Michel confirmed to us that he had seen numerous recoveries that took place in record time and that he had healed wounds in a single session, while the patient had been in psychotherapeutic treatment for years.

It seems as if the tapping bypasses our emotions, which are generators of limiting beliefs, to directly address the brain. To better summarize EFT, I like to use the following metaphor. In South America, the famous Iguazu Falls are visible from Argentina and Brazil. To get from the Argentinian side to the Brazilian side, a distance of about a hundred meters as the crow flies, you must walk around an edge of nearly one hundred kilometers. If the body and the brain are the two sides, the traditional psychotherapeutic path corresponds to the long detour, while EFT is a bridge between the two sides.

EFT is simple to understand, learn and master. Once getting over the bizarre impression that comes from tapping on different places on the body, while alternating between critical sentences (for example, "Despite the fact that I am fat") and kind ones (for example, "I love myself and I accept myself") about yourself, the emotions begin to let go, tears flow, anger, sadness, shame, fear come out more or less violently… Then the healing happens, the sky of feelings clears up, anger, sadness, shame and fear disappear and the session concludes. Sometimes the first session is the last. Two or three one-hour sessions suffice, even in difficult cases.

According to psychotherapist Helena Fone, if EFT enables the treatment of numerous emotional, physical and psychological hardships, overcoming numerous dependencies (tobacco, alcohol, gambling, food, sex) and bad habits, it is a fantastic booster for the development of physical and psychological performances, used for example by golf champions to maximize their concentration or by students to prepare for exams. You will find numerous references to EFT at the end of her book (Fone, 2008), or on the internet.

c. Cardiac coherence

Cardiac coherence is a simple, extremely efficient technique for preventing and managing stress. It comes from the works of a group of clinicians that were associated with Doc Childre in the United States during the beginning of the 1990s (Childre & Martin, 2000). It synchronizes your heart and your brain using a tailored breathing rhythm.

Our autonomic nervous system, which regulates all of the autonomous functions of the body (breathing, visual accommodation, digestive system, the growth of body and head hair…) has two sub-systems: the sympathetic system and the parasympathetic system, whose stable functioning is vital for life. An imbalance in this functioning can result in serious pathological consequences.

The sympathetic system is similar to an accelerator because it does everything possible for a leak: it accelerates the cardiac rate, contracts the arteries, dilates the pupils, makes breathing faster and slows down the digestive transit. Conversely, the parasympathetic system acts like a break and allows for recovery: it slows down the heart, releases the arteries, contracts the pupils, makes breathing slower and accelerates the digestive transit (Cungi & Deglon, 2009).

This regulation happens automatically, unconsciously, and is beyond our control.

In stressful situations, one of the two systems prevails over the other and an imbalance sets in that, if continued over the long-term, can lead to serious disorders, chronic conditions, even cardiovascular incidents or cancer. Synchronization cannot be reestablished by will. But it can be reestablished in a natural and rapid way through breathing. By breathing at a certain rate (corresponding to the resonance rate of the aorta) the two systems regulate themselves and calm returns within a few seconds. You just need to inhale five seconds and exhale five seconds. An inhaling/exhaling cycle lasts therefore ten seconds and there are six cycles per minute. This is called breathing at rate six.

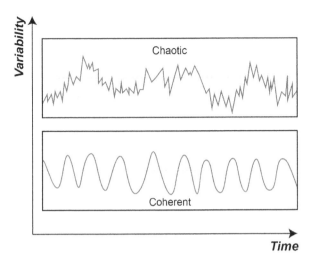

Cardiac Coherence

This return to balance is represented by the variation of your heart rate. Assume that your rate is 75 beats per minute. This rate is never strictly fixed: when you are resting, your heart rate varies in a disorderly way around 75 (i.e. 78, 73, 69, 77, 84, 69…). When you are in a state of stress, your heart rate increases, going for example, up to 100, and its fluctuation becomes quite chaotic: 75, 90, 125, 100, 110, 85, 83, 107, 125… In fact, the more the fluctuation of your heart rate is chaotic, the more your two systems, sympathetic and parasympathetic, are out of synch, and your metabolism becomes unbalanced.

However, as soon as you breathe at rate six, the fluctuation in your heart rate becomes sinusoidal: 75, 77, 79, 77, 75, 73, 71, 73, 75… In a few seconds this breathing resynchronizes your sympathetic and parasympathetic systems and re-establishes the balance of your metabolism. Doing this kind of breathing for three to five minutes rebalances your body for several hours. In addition, the more often you practice rate six breathing, the better your heart will support big fluctuations in its cardiac rate: 75, 90, 105, 90, 75, 60, 45, 60, 75… By increasing the range of its cardiac rate variability, your heart learns to quickly find a balance from significant extreme values.

Cardiac coherence is excellent for preparing for a situation that you know is stressful for you: speaking in public, defending an unpopular idea, having a difficult face-to-face interview, etc. In these cases, a few minutes before entering the situation, practice breathing at rate six for two or three minutes. The fluctuation of your heart rate will become sinusoidal, the sympathetic and parasympathetic systems will synchronize with each other, and calm will set in immediately, lasting for one to two hours.

Introducing cardiac coherence in your everyday life soothes your mood all day long by practicing it every time possible, or as soon as you feel the need, anywhere you are: in the car, at the office, on the bus, walking… The opportunities are endless for adding these three minutes easily into your daily life.

In the case of sudden, unexpected and brutal stress, a variation, called the calm crisis, consists of inhaling while counting to three, blocking your breathing for three seconds, then exhaling for three seconds (Cungi, 2003).

For myself, I couple the body scan with cardiac coherence by proceeding in the following way. As I am used to breathing at rate six, this breathing mode is maintained automatically when I begin. So I just need to proceed to mindfulness meditation based on the body scan while breathing at rate six. So I get the benefits of mindfulness meditation coupled with those of cardiac coherence, for fifteen minutes. In terms of cardiac coherence, this is a long time. I can therefore feel the benefits for about four hours.

d. The Enneagram

Throughout this book I have spoken extensively about the pertinence of the Enneagram as a tool for self-knowledge. It is also a very powerful tool for self-development. Your Enneatype is the key to understanding your basic functioning and underlying motivations that drive you. By linking your enneatype to your wings and your arrows, the dynamic of the Enneagram model suggests resources that you can call upon to support and develop what is best in you, and make you attentive to the bad habits, limiting beliefs, negative or even self-destructive behaviors, of your blockage zone.

No matter which path you take, the Enneagram allows you to become yourself in the richest, most complete and well-rounded sense that you decide to be.

Key take-aways

- Love yourself with clarity, kindness and support

- To be in good physical shape, follow the rules for getting good sleep, eating healthy and regularly practicing a simple activity (the sun salutation, the balance exercise…) and get an annual check-up

- To ensure your mental shape, practice the body scan, write three positive events daily and educate yourself

- To manage your emotions, practice cardiac coherence each day and use EFT

- To manage your relationships with others, use non-violent communication

- To develop yourself, use the Enneagram

- Remind yourself that "Happiness is wellbeing that we are conscious of"

CHAPTER 8

FOCUS, FOCUS AND... FOCUS

In 1906, the Italian sociologist and economist Vilfredo Pareto observed that 20% of the population possessed 80% of Italy's wealth. The observation that approximately 80% of effects were produced by approximately 20% of the causes had been made in many other situations, which led to Pareto's 80/20 Principle. Of course, this principle is totally empirical and can only be proven approximately. But the rule has the merit of highlighting the importance of focusing on the essential, on the 20% of efforts that produce 80% of the results, and ignoring the unnecessary, the 80% of efforts that only bring the remaining 20%.

In order to become an excellent salesperson, focus on your strengths, your client and your plan.

Focus on your strengths

We have examined your strengths throughout earlier chapters. You know them and you have inventoried them. Choose 20% of your strengths and skills, those that make you reach 80% of your results and focus on them. It is essential to develop and strengthen them to bring them to a still higher level of performance. If you focus on your strengths you will become stronger; if you focus on your weaknesses you will become less mediocre.

Focus on the essential for your client

Focus on the business that makes sense for them. If it makes sense for them, it will make sense for your company and for you. The reverse is not necessarily true. Out of all the projects that interest them, identify, with their help, the 20% that *really* make sense for their business, the 20% for which they are ready to pay a premium, to move heaven and earth to succeed, to call you on the weekend to know where things are with the project.

Focus on your plan

First of all, structure your territory according to Pareto's rule: classify your clients based on the turnover they bring you, and segment them into two categories, the 20% that bring you the most and the 80% others. My experience has taught me that approximately 20% to 25% of my clients bring me effectively between 70% and 80% of my sales. I therefore dedicate my time *proportionally* to those that bring sales in, that is 80% of my time spent with the first 20% and 20% spent with the rest. These figures are not universal. Adapt them to your territory, based on the dynamic in your industry, the life-cycle of your products, and your experience. They serve to illustrate the basic idea which is to focus on what is essential in your current business, while keeping an eye on what could become your business tomorrow or after tomorrow. Re-do this exercise at the beginning of each year and readjust your territory accordingly.

Then, establish your plan of action. To do this, imagine that your territory is a blank white board, attached to the wall and your actions are nails. Certain parts of the board are extremely hard and others are much softer. Your objective is to hammer the nails in as deeply as possible in a limited amount of time. You can do this in two ways: either compulsively, pounding on many nails, at a furious pace, anywhere, anyhow; or in a focused manner, one by one, in the right place, with the right amount of strength. There are many salespeople who take on too many projects, reply to too many requests, solicitations, calls for tender, trying to hammer in as many nails as possible without discrimination. Sometimes this comes from a need to show, to oneself or to others, that they are active; often, it's bad sales organization. By planning your priorities, your projects and your actions, by leaving some space for the unforeseen, by dedicating time to explore and analyze new opportunities, you will know which nail to hammer, why, when, and how.

The three sales rhythms

Three rhythms intervene in your sales process:

- Your client's, according to their priorities, the number of decision makers involved and their decision process timeframe

- Your company's, according to the priorities of the units concerned, their processes, the availability of your colleagues, your hierarchy and those that are involved in the approval process

- Your own, according to your personal priorities, your own way of working and your motivation

Many salespeople believe that they mainly depend on their client. This is a limiting belief. In fact, your power of influence on the three rhythms is bigger than it appears.

To move your sales project forward, assume that you are able to influence: a) your client 30%, thanks to your regular contacts, the collaboration established between your teams and the dynamic that you bring; b) your company 50%, thanks to your role and your leadership; c) you 100%, thanks to your motivation and your ability to advance. This means that you have control over $(30+50+100)/300 = 180/300 = 60\%$ of the sales process. While your client and your company controls, between the two, the remaining $40\% = (70+50)/300$.

The goal of this simple calculation is not to quantify to the exact percentage point who manages the sales process but to sensitize you to the fact that you can influence the process a lot more than you think. When you feel like the progress is stagnating, use this to understand why and to identify which factors should be reinforced. This reinforcement might need to happen in yourself. It can also take place internally – within your company, your hierarchy and your teams – or externally, with your client and their teams. This approach should reassure you by showing you, in a pragmatic way, that your leadership really can make the difference.

Are you the Hare or the Tortoise? No. Be the Hare and the Tortoise!

Two French sayings that make very good sense are the foundation for proper management of the sales pace:

- "When it's time, it's time; before time is not on time; after time, is no longer on time", said 19th-century poet and songwriter Jules Jouy;

- "There is no point in running, you need to leave on time". The 17th century poet, Jean de la Fontaine, concluded his famous fable "The Hare and the Tortoise" with these words.

These sayings will help you conserve your energy during most of your time in order to expend it at the right moment. My experience allowed me to observe that the best way to manage the sales process is based on:

- "Walking" 60% of the time, that is, about three days per week

- "Long-distance racing" 30% of the time, or a day and a half per week

- "Sprinting" 10% of the time, or a half day per week

What I mean by this is that for half of the time it is not worth running around in all directions, trying to hammer 36,000 nails right and left, exhausting yourself by thinking that you are not doing enough. Personally, I spend half of my time observing and listening, to understand my clients, learn about new sectors, new technologies, develop my network and to ask for advice from both my clients and my colleagues. That is to say, living 50% of the time without stress. It is what I call walking and its goal is to prepare you.

Because, when an opportunity appears on the horizon, when a specific need or concrete project is identified and discussed, it is time to begin the long-distance race and start the marathon. This marathon is not run alone but in teams. Everyone starts to sharpen their tools, the specialists consolidate technical information, the lawyers begin to study different types of contracts, management starts asking questions, the light signals change to orange, and meetings with the client take place more frequently.

Finally we receive the call for tender. The team has between two and five weeks to respond and win. The sprint begins. A few light signals change to green, others remain orange and some persistently stay red. You need to refocus, motivate, call for help, insist, and escalate to your hierarchy, moving heaven and earth to make everyone sprint in the right direction. It is at the moment of the sprint that working in pairs, in tandem, takes on its importance: having a sparring partner to rapidly confront and challenge your ideas and propositions, a "business confidant" who knows the file to share your doubts and concerns, a back-up in case you are absent, due to sickness or something else, are a few of the advantages of sprinting in pairs. The principle of synergy, according to which "1 + 1 = 3" is so appropriate, especially under time pressure.

Focus your life on the essential

In the first chapter, we addressed the importance of aligning your Life Apartment with your priorities, which take place in different areas: family, professional, social, personal, spiritual and other. There is a big risk of wanting to do too much, to be overwhelmed, to drown in the details and lose sight of the essential. Also, establish four to five important life goals. For each one of them, build your

GOPA tree and select three objectives to reach for the year. This represents twelve to fifteen annual objectives. Which is more than enough! Then, identify the projects that last from two to six months whose results are crucial to achieving your objectives, and finally, stay connected to these projects daily by accomplishing each day an action linked to your four to five important life goals. By advancing each day, even small steps, toward your important goals, you will reach them without realizing it, and without leaving one by the wayside. However, reject everything that does not go in the same direction as your goals. Stick to the essential.

Key take-aways

- Focus on :

    - 20% of your strengths: those that are essential for you

    - 20% of your projects: those that really make sense for your client

    - 20% of your clients: those that generate 80% of your turnover

- Segment your territory according to the 20/80 principle

- You have more influence on the sales process than you think

- Remember that in sales:

    - When it's time, it's time; before time is not on time; after time, is no longer on time

    - There is no point in running, you need to leave on time

- Stick to the essential

AND NOW?

Thank you for taking the time to read this book. It is more difficult to conclude a book that it seems. For weeks, I thought about you, writing what will take you a few hours to read and a few years to put into practice. We have looked at numerous areas of your personal development and encountered several tools that will serve you as much in your life as in your noble profession as a salesperson. It is up to you to choose the ones that work for you, make them your own, sharpen them and integrate them into your daily practice. No matter what, if I was able, even in the slightest way, to inspire you to want to take charge of your life, to know why you do what you do, to be proud to be a salesperson, to flourish in this marvelous profession because it is rich with encounters, challenges and accomplishments, to show you how sales is like coaching your clients when it relies on sincere, respectful and empathetic support, to take care of your mind, your emotions and your body, and finally to focus on the essential things in your life and your profession, then I will have the humble feeling of having done useful work.

A last word: your comments, suggestions and experiences interest me. In order to prolong this discussion, please share them with me by writing to guy@anastazebusinesscoaching. com. I thank you in advance.

SUGGESTIONS FOR FURTHER READING

Achor, S. (2011). *The Happiness Advantage: The Seven Principles of Positive Psychology that Fuel Success and Performance at Work.* Virgin Books

Anastaze, G. (2014). *The Utility of Enneagram in Executive Coaching.* Master Thesis. Executive Coaching Master Program, University Cergy-Pontoise, France

Baghai, M., Coley, S. & White D. (2000). *The Alchemy of Growth.* Basic Books

Ben-Shahar, T. (2008). *Happier: Can you learn to be Happy?* McGraw-Hill

Ben-Shahar, T. (2014). *Choose the Life You Want: The Mindful Way to Happiness.* Experiment LLC

Boniwell, I. (2012). *Positive Psychology in a Nutshell: The Science of Happiness.* Open University Press. 3rd Edition

Boniwell, I. *Positran Strengths Cards.* http://www.acukltd.com/cards/

Bregman, P. (2012). *18 Minutes: Find Your Focus, Master Distraction and Get the Right Things Done.* Orion

Hefferon, K. & Boniwell, I. (2011). *Positive Psychology. Theory, Research and Application.* Open University Press

Craig G. (2011). *The EFT Manual.* Energy Psychology Press, 2nd Ed.

Cungi, C. (2003). *Savoir gérer son stress en toutes circonstances.* Paris: Retz

Cungi, C. (2006). *L'alliance thérapeutique*. Paris: Retz

Cungi, C. & Deglon, C. (2009). *Cohérence Cardiaque, Nouvelles techniques pour faire face au stress.* Paris: Retz

Daniels, D. & Price, V. (2009). *Essential Enneagram: The Definitive Personality Test and Self-Discovery Guide*. HarperOne, Rev. Ed.

Childre D. & Martin H. (2000). *The HeartMath Solution*. HarperOne

Fagioli, M.-C. (2002). *Coaching, vous avez dit coaching?* Grolley: Les Editions de l'Hèbe

Fagioli, M.-C. (2007). *À quoi sert l'Ennéagramme?* Grolley: Les Editions de l'Hèbe

Falcao, H. (2010). *Value Negotiation*. Pearson Education South Asia

Fone, H. (2008). *Emotional Freedom Technique For Dummies*. John Wiley & Sons

Frankl, V. (2000). *Recollections: An Autobiography*. Basic Books

Frankl, V. (2004). *Man's Search for Meaning.* Rider, New Edition

Frankl, V. (2014). *The Will to Meaning: Foundations and Applications of Logotherapy*. Plume Books, Expanded Edition

Giroud, F. (1972). *Si je mens*. Editions Stock

Kabat-Zinn, J. (2004). *Wherever You Go, There You Are: Mindfulness meditation for everyday life*. Piatkus

Kabat-Zinn, J. (2005). *Guided Mindfulness Meditation Audio CD*. Sounds True Inc

Kilburg, R. R. (2000). *Executive Coaching: Developing Managerial Wisdom in a World of Chaos*. Washington DC: American Psychological Association.

La Fontaine, J. de. (2007). *The Complete Fables of Jean de La Fontaine*. University of Illinois Press

Lapid-Bogda, G. (2007). *What type of leader are you? Using the Enneagram System to Identify and Grow Your Leadership Strengths and Achieve Maximum Success*. New York: McGraw Hill

Lyubomirsky, S. (2013) *The Myths of Happiness: What Should Make You Happy, But Doesn't, What Shouldn't Make You Happy, But Does*. Penguin Books

Madanes, Y. & R. (2011). *From Stuckness to Growth. Enneagram coaching*. CreateSpace Independent Publishing Platform, Amazon.co.uk Ltd

Miller, W.R. & Rollnick, S. (2012). *Motivational Interviewing: Helping People Change*. Guilford Press. 3rd Edition

Palmer, H. (1991). *The Enneagram: Understanding Yourself and Others in Your Life*. Thorsons

Palmer, H. (1996). *Enneagram in Love and Work: Understanding Your Intimate and Business Relationships*. Harper Collins

Piazza, O. (2011). *Using Motivational Interviewing in Executive Coaching: Principles, Techniques, Purpose, Indications, Key Success Factors*. Master Thesis. Executive Coaching Master Program, University Cergy-Pontoise, France

Pralong, J. (2009). *Apprivoiser son caractère*. Editions des Béatitudes

Rosenberg, M. B. (2003). *Nonviolent Communication: a Language of Life*. Puddle Dancer Press. 2nd Revised Edition

Sander, D. & Scherer, K. (2014). *Oxford Companion to Emotion and the Affective Sciences*. Oxford University Press

Saint Exupéry, A. de (2001). *The Little Prince*. Egmont

Schein. E. (2011). *Helping: How to Offer, Give, and Receive Help*. Berrett-Koehler

Schein, E. (2013). *Humble Inquiry: The Gentle Art of Asking Instead of Telling*. Berrett-Koehler

Seligman, M. (2011). *Flourish: A New Understanding of Happiness and Well-Being—and How To Achieve Them*. Nicholas Brealey Publishing

ACKNOWLEDGMENTS

This book is the result of the extraordinary sum of rich and intense exchanges, mutual support, overcome obstacles, shared moments, active listening, knowledge passed on and reciprocal kindness with hundreds of clients, business partners, mentors, colleagues, teachers, coaches and my family.

My clients, some of whom have become close friends, are the *raison d'être* of this book.

Thank you to:

- Dieter Denger for his "trouble-shooting" project in Asia with its stressful beginnings, achieved with success and celebrated at the Sydney Opera;

- Georges Diserens for having shown me how to manage the most complex of business matters with unequalled wisdom and pragmatism;

- Jean-Claude Favre, who is a man of his word, total commitment and absolute rigor;

- Dr. Chris Jones who is as at ease in physics as he is in business;

- Jean-Pierre Michel who taught me how to take your time in order to accomplish great things;

- Halim Tabet for having shown me how challenging it is to negotiate with an Afro-Lebanese and how beautiful a country Senegal is;

- Alexandre Vassiltchikov with whom a real partnership was built, first on a genuine alliance, then on shared principles and finally on a shared desire to succeed;

- Peter Wintsch, whose relentless expectations are only matched by his warm generosity.

To hire a theoretical physicist who wanted to work in sales was a bold gamble for Raphaël Brunner, Director of IBM Swiss Romande. Thank you Raphaël for having dared to give me this magnificent opportunity. IBM is an immense pool of great salespeople and remarkable leaders. Many of those I collaborated with share a real passion for the client. Thank you to:

- Henry R. Brandt, Pasquale Di Cesare and Michel Roethlisberger for those wonderful moments when we knew that we were building cathedrals with our client;

- David Cremese for your sound advice, and providing serenity, intelligence and depth;

- Nicholas Donofrio for your inspiration and precious lessons each time we met. A five minute conversation with you is a master class in leadership all by itself;

- Claudio de Franchi for your example to bounce back and go where you want;

- Philippe Froté for often having won thanks to your unbelievably creative offers;

- Edward Gaehwiler for your sponsorship, your foreword in this book and for sharing common values as much on a personal level as professional;

- Eva-Helen Inwyler, Sandy Gros-Louis and Brigitte Le Moine for having given me the opportunity to collaborate with the most efficient women's Dream Team that I have ever met.

- Herbert B. Kaestner for having been a master of sales. I observed and accompanied you for one year when I first started. Thank you Herbert for having guided me and shown me how to develop a sales relationship that is sincere and for the very, very long-term;

- Christian Keller for your confidence and your unwavering professional support;

- Hans-Ulrich Maerki for having been an extraordinary leader and mentor, for having helped me question myself and find meaning in what I was doing;

- Demetrio Mafrica for your warm humour, generosity and listening to the client first;

- Mark Mullins for five years of intense and fruitful collaboration;

- Bruno Poussard for having placed your trust in me and given me the opportunity to help you grow your team;

- Peter Quadri for your remarkable role model as manager, leader and mentor;

- Tony Reis for knowing how to put people at the heart of the company when you transformed it and for a conversation at The Hotel Bristol Geneva that changed my career;

- Yvonne Sala for having always been there since the first day;

- Nicole Seeberger for your desire to win, your pugnacity and your optimism;

- Dr. Hans Ruedi Sprenger for our conversations centered on what makes sense for our clients;

- Shahab M. Syed for our discussions about all types of architecture, including those of the Supreme Architect;

- Roland Tissot for being one of the best project managers I have ever met and for your sharp sense of humor;

- Olivier Vareilhes for your trust, support and our complicity in the approach to sales in general, and to clients, in particular.

Thank you also to:

- Marc Chikhani, CEO SR Operations, for the pleasure of working together and discovering the cafes of Carouge;

- Eric Guinchard, CEO Wird, for your contagious optimism, your business sense and entrepreneurial spirit;

- Eric Robert, for your exceptional understanding of the customer relationship, for being the best car salesperson I know and for having known how to make me wait patiently… for one year before receiving the car of my dreams;

I had the good fortune of getting acquainted with, learning and putting into practice the approaches presented in this book with enthusiastic and passionate teachers, scientists and practitioners.

Thank you to:

- Prof. Guido Bondolfi, Associate Professor of Psychiatry at the Faculty of Medicine of the University of Geneva, for having welcomed me for eight weeks in the Mindfulness-Based Stress Reduction (MBSR) program that he directs at the University Hospitals of Geneva;

- Dr. Ilona Boniwell, CEO Positran and Director of International MSc in Applied Positive Psychology at Anglia Ruskin University in the UK, and Associate professor at Ecole Centrale Paris, for your brilliant teaching on positive psychology. You gave me the keys to structure, understand and develop the best we have inside us;

- Dr. Charly Cungi, Psychiatrist, Cognitive Behavioral Therapy (CBT) specialist, for your numerous practical and accessible books, and your outstanding teaching on CBT applied to coaching;

- Marie-Claire Fagioli, Coach and consultant, pioneer of the Enneagram in Swiss Romande, for having helped me discover the subtle intricacies of the Enneagram and integrating them into my coaching practice;

- Jean-Michel Gurret, Therapist and trainer, pioneer of Emotional Freedom Techniques

(EFT) in France, for having introduced me to EFT, an approach that is definitely surprising and incredibly efficient;

- Dr. Philippe Kehrer for teaching me how to manage my sleep thanks to CBT. Thank you so much!

- Olivier Piazza, Co-Director of the Executive Coaching Master Program at University of Cergy Pontoise, France, for being a great coach and an excellent teacher. Your active listening, your kind humility, your "straight to the point" advice, are sources of inspiration for the coaching community and for your students. Thank you for being my friend;

- Charlotte Tracewski, FSP Psychologist (The Federation of Swiss Psychologists) at Neuro-Edu-Action Practice, for having taught me to untie myself from all special diets and to manage my nutrition with CBT;

- The teachers of the Executive Coaching Master Program: Patrick Amar, Dr. François Balta, Odile Bernhardt, Roland Brunner, Prof. Florence Daumarie, Jean-Luc Ewald, Dr. Richard Kilburg, Dr. Michel Moral, Philippe Rosinski and Dr. Jean-Jacques Wittezaele, who shared with me their coaching methods, procedures and points of view with passion. The outcome is a great asset of diversity, synergy and differences, and the desire to further examine these various facets of the same diamond that is Executive Coaching;

- My classmates and in particular: Marc Blaise, Karine Castello, Elee Duconseille, Jocelyne Gaston, Béatrice Gensous, Florent Ladrech, Florent Métivet and Pascale Richard for the great pleasure of having shared our discoveries, our questioning and our projects;

- Christophe Ameline, Sakina Aubert, Laura Bacci, Henri Cnops, Michel del Pino, Chris Hunsicker, Sonia Gavira, Thomas Gelmi, Nathalie Lalande, Olivier Piazza, Julien Soive and Jean-François Vleugels, members of the international community of Ford Consumer Experience Movement coaches, for your Jazz Team spirit, our extraordinarily rich discussions, and the shared pleasure of helping our coachees restore meaning to their profession, recover wellbeing and gain greater autonomy;

This book would not have been possible without the support and the contribution of the following people.

Thank you very much to:

- Catherine Besenwald, for your creativity and your illustrations;

- Neil Coe, for having designed the cover of the book in great harmony with its spirit;

- Mindy Gibbins-Klein, The Book Midwife, for being an incredible coach. Your precious advice on the art of writing, your practical and methodical approach, your persistent drive and your kind patience allowed me to overcome the challenges of writing this book during a turning point in my life. Thanks to you, I was able to experience Mark Twain's motto: "They didn't know it was impossible, so they did it";

- Julia Motet and Marianne Scheer, for their excellent translation, as well as for our pleasant and smooth collaboration;

- My panel of readers: Dr. Karine Anastaze-Stelle, David Cremese, Thomas Cremese, Anissa Desuzinge, Julien Dubrez, Julien Gaillard, Eric Guinchard, Brigitte Le Moine, Demetrio Mafrica, Lisa Neddam, Nicole Seeberger and Olivier Vareilhes for your time, your wise and useful feedback, your "out of the box" ideas and suggestions and for sharing your personal and professional experiences;

Finally, I thank, from the bottom of my heart, those that contributed, and contribute to, who I am by nourishing my *savoir-être* with their love, the heritage of certain values, their presence, their joy of life and their help in making me reassess myself, day after day, in order to let go and concentrate on the essential.

Thank you to:

- Renée, my mother, for having taken care of so many things without me realizing it, for having taught me to smile and to love others, and for the extraordinary gift of having waited for me before leaving;

- René, my father, for having taught me to believe in myself, to think and to love numbers, the piano and jazz, and for having supported me in many of my choices;

- Henri, my brother, for having taught me that you must love others while they are in this world;

- Claudia, the mother of my daughters for being a super Mom and for having shared wonderful moments together;

- Brigitte, my life partner, for your unfailing support, your unwavering optimism and your gentle life style;

- Karine, my oldest daughter, for being how you are, your presence and determination, for your taste for action and reflection in the assistance that you give to your little patients, your family and friends, and for having given birth, with your husband, Dr. Marc Stelle, to a little David with a mischievous smile;

- Alexandra, my youngest daughter, for being how you are, for your sparkle and your empathy, and for knowing how to find the right words that heal the soul and let in the sun;

- And David, my grandson, for having made me revisit my priorities and for giving me, every Monday afternoon, happiness and the sense for enjoying the present moment by your side.

ABOUT THE AUTHOR

Guy Anastaze is an expert in business efficiency, behavioral and relational aspects of business performance, and improving the customer experience. Combining 30 years of sales management experience at IBM with his passion for people, Guy coaches senior executives in their managerial practice, decision-making and career management. He also supports sales teams in developing long-term business strategies, effective management of their commercial relations and increasing their sales performance. Guy's approach is to strengthen the capacity of participants' individual and collective transformation through strong knowledge of human functioning based on positive psychology, cognitive and behavioral techniques, the systemic approach and the Enneagram.

Franco–Swiss, Guy was born in Bordeaux (France), grew up in Buenos Aires (Argentina) and lives in Geneva (Switzerland). He has two lovely daughters and a grandson, born during the writing of this book. He enjoys playing jazz piano, composing tangos, and relaxing in the Alps.

Guy is the founder and CEO of Anastaze Business Coaching Sàrl. He graduated in Executive Coaching from the University of Cergy Pontoise (France), has an MBA from IMD Lausanne, a PhD in Theoretical Physics from the University of Geneva, a Doctorate 3rd Cycle from the University of Strasbourg and a chemical engineering degree from the Ecole Nationale Supérieure de Chimie de Mulhouse (France). He is author of a number of scientific and business publications, including a treatise on "Artificial Intelligence: A Strategic Choice for Corporations." Prior to joining IBM, he completed research projects at the Center of Nuclear Research in Strasbourg, at the Ecole Polytechnique in Paris, and at the University of Geneva.

Guy Anastaze is available for coaching and select speaking engagements. For inquires or to share reader feedback contact: guy@anastazebusinesscoaching.com

Lightning Source UK Ltd.
Milton Keynes UK
UKOW06f1237190416

272530UK00007B/132/P